"This book isn't just for triathletes; it will be priceless for anyone wanting to swim freestyle better. Terry Laughlin's guidance has transformed the swimming experience for me. My stroke feels smoother and more powerful at age 45 than when I was setting world records as a 15-year old. And it has helped me to convey things I did instinctively as an elite swimmer, but could never before put into words, to the swimmers and triathletes I coach. Finally it has given me a much more eloquent "body language" in the water. I feel wiser because of it!"

Shane Gould
11-time World Record holder,
5-time Olympic medalist,
Masters and open-water swimmer.
Total Immersion Coach

"Terry has a remarkable gift for conveying swimming insights for all ages and abilities, from beginners to elites. Since attending a TI clinic and reading *Triathlon Swimming Made Easy*, I now focus on Fishlike swimming, instead of grinding out yardage. In college, I trained over 50,000 yards a week. After just 8 months of practicing only 15,000 yards a week, I am swimming freestyle faster than in college! I'm no longer afraid to swim slowly in practice, as long as I have perfect technique. I never fully understood or appreciated technique before. Now I teach it to everyone!"

Susie Stark
First Lieutenant, USMC
Professional Triathlete
Resident Triathlon Team Member,
U.S. Olympic Training Center

"As a beginner, swimming is by far the most challenging aspect of triathlon for me. During my first race, I swam hard just trying to get to the bike and run. But watching a few swimmers glide effortlessly through the water convinced me there must be an easier way. Terry gave me a sneak peek at his book and it made an immediate difference. This book will truly help you swim more efficiently and effortlessly than ever before."

Gregg A. Wheeler
Age group triathlete

"Poor swimming always held me back from realizing my multisport dream and the absence of practical, triathlon-specific swimming information was just as frustrating. With this book, in twelve weeks I went from struggling through a few 100's to finishing my first Olympic distance triathlon with astonishing ease. I have never been so excited reading any genre of book before and I thank Terry for helping me reach my goals faster than I ever thought possible."

Tim Rooney
Age group triathlete

"How I wish I'd had this book years ago. I always finished the swim leg in the lead, but working so hard to be there made the bike and run an ordeal. These days, having learned to swim effortlessly, I finish my open water swims at the front of the pack and I'm not even breathing hard! This book is a priceless primer on how to do it the right way."

Beth O'Connor Baker
Masters Swimming World Record Holder
National Triathlon Sprint Champion
& USAT World Team Member

"This book provides a practical, do-it-yourself guide for applying the TI method to open water swimming. Terry has solved one of the most enigmatic problems of triathlon: how to transform the swim from a gruesome struggle against the water into a relaxed, pleasurable experience. This will be a great confidence builder for triathletes."

Ivar Brinkman
Certified Triathlon Coach
The Netherlands

"If you are serious about reaching your highest athletic potential as a triathlete, buy *Triathlon Swimming Made Easy*. Whether you race sprint or ironman distance, this book will help you become a graceful, balanced and faster swimmer. It's the triathlete's self-mastery guide for swimming."

Mark Wilson
USAT Certified Coach,
Total Immersion Certified Coach

"After attending a TI triathlon camp in Vermont in August of 2000, I have completely transformed my swimming, resulting in a phenomenal increase in my efficiency and a steady improvement in my swim time. I now swim with much less effort and much more confidence. TI has also changed my priorities. I used to train. Now I practice and am focused totally on attaining Mastery. I look forward to a lifetime of satisfying drilling and practice."

Andy Robinson
T.I. Alum, Age group triathlete

"My goal for my first Ironman was to finish, to enjoy the experience, and to race as efficiently as possible. Using TI techniques for all of my swim training made for an enjoyable swim that was relaxed and smooth despite 1800+ churning swimmers. Feeling fresh upon exiting the water certainly made the next 112 miles on the bike, and 26.2 miles on the run easier and the finish line that much closer."

Ed Colet
Age group triathlete

"Terry Laughlin understands triathlon racing! *Triathlon Swimming Made Easy* is the complete package for improving the swim leg of a triathlon while conserving energy for improved performance in cycling and running as well. It offers powerful, immediately-effective improvement techniques for the novice and the experienced triathlete."

John Fisher
T.I. Alum, Age group triathlete

"I am a 49 year old who began competing in Triathlons for the first time this year with absolutely no experience swimming. In fact, I could not swim 50 yards non-stop! As a result of learning and following the TI method, I completed 7 triathlons between May and September. The swim has changed from something that was totally intimidating to the part of triathlon that I most enjoy. In fact, I was able to complete a 5K open water swim in September. Thank you, Terry, for helping me and thousands of others to conquer their fears and discover the excitement and satisfaction of a new sport!"

Steve A. Gooch
Age group triathlete

"I recommend this book to anyone who wants to learn to swim more efficiently. When I started swimming a year ago I couldn't swim 100 meters. In my last race, thanks to TI, I was 3rd out of the water for my age group!!"

Judy Doherty
Age group triathlete

"Why not finally read, feel, and flow in the postmodern glide of swimming? Terry Laughlin, in his new book, once again gives us unique insight into this art. Flow, balance, "strokes of languid purpose," a "Lance Armstrong in the water playing gear games," Enter the new triathlon millenium as a Fishlike swimmer."

Corinne Machoud Nivon
USAT certified coach,
Mexican triathlon certified coach,
TI certified coach
Age group "postmodern" triathlete.

"*Triathlon Swimming Made Easy* can turn ANYONE into a beautiful, Fishlike freestyler. It helped me to my best season of open-water swimming in 30 years. Swimming the TI way has become a source of endless pleasure for me and it will for you too."

Don Walsh
TI-certified coach,
Champion Marathon Swimmer

Triathlon Swimming Made Easy

Also by Terry Laughlin:

Books:

The Swimmer's Bible

The Swiminar Workbook

The Guide to Fishlike Swimming

Total Immersion: The Revolutionary Way to Swim Better, Faster, and Easier

Swimming Made Easy: The Total Immersion Way for Any Swimmer to Achieve Fluency, Ease, and Speed in Any Stroke

The Total Immersion Pool Primer: Freestyle and Backstroke

The Total Immersion Pool Primer: Butterfly and Breaststroke

Videos:

Freestyle and Backstroke: The Total Immersion Way

Butterfly and Breaststroke: The Total Immersion Way

Fishlike Freestyle: The Total Immersion Way

Triathlon Swimming Made Easy

How *ANYONE* Can Succeed in Triathlon (or Open-Water Swimming) with *Total Immersion*

TM

Terry Laughlin

Total Immersion, Inc.
New Paltz, NY

ISBN: 1-9310009-03-1

For more information about Terry Laughlin's Total Immersion swim workshops, call 800-609-7946 (845-256-9770 from outside the USA).

Text and concept: Terry Laughlin
Editing: Barbara Tomchin and John Delves
Design, graphics, and technical contributor: Glenn Mills
Production: Tara Laughlin

Published by Total Immersion, Inc.
171 Main Street
New Paltz, NY 12561

First edition published 2002
Printed in the United States of America

10 9 8 7 6 5 4 3 2 1

This is for Alice, the most generous and caring person I know and my precious partner in life.
She makes it all possible.

Contents

Acknowledgments

Joe Friel and Lew Kidder shared priceless insights into the sport of triathlon.

All my Total Immersion coaching colleagues helped build "buzz" for TI among triathletes.

Bill Russell allowed us to use the Moriello Pool in New Paltz for photos used herein.

Thanks to Shane Gould, Barbara Tomchin, Kermit Hummel and Rob Lias for demonstrating drills and open water techniques.

Thanks to Joshua Gold, Carol Charbono and Bob Wiskera for demonstrating the exercises in Chapter 19.

Glenn Mills, Barbara Tomchin, Tara Laughlin and John Delves turned my words into a book. Thanks to all.

And, as ever, thanks to Fiona, Cari and Betsy for humoring — and occasionally sharing — my lifelong swimming immersion.

Introduction

Why You Are About to Become a Transformed Swimmer!

In 1989, I began teaching adult swimmers at Total Immersion summer camps and was soon teaching a few hundred improvement-minded swimmers each year. Early on, few were triathletes; we were teaching all four strokes and triathletes were mainly interested in freestyle. In 1991 I began writing for Triathlon Today magazine (now called Inside Triathlon) and began to see so many triathletes at my swim camps that, in 1993, we began offering freestyle-only programs. Triathletes flocked to these workshops and I recognized their powerful hunger for instruction in swimming technique.

In 1995 I published a book called *Total Immersion: The Revolutionary Way to Swim Better, Faster, and Easier*, which quickly became the best-selling book on swimming. Though I didn't write this book specifically for triathletes, thousands of multi-sporters made it their swimming bible and the number of triathletes attending TI workshops exploded.

Teaching thousands of triathletes has convinced me that *swimming for triathlon* (and swimming in open water) is a significantly different sport than competitive swimming (as in age-group, high-school, college, and Masters meets). While most triathletes copy the training programs of competitive swimmers, they shouldn't. Here's why:

- Competitive swimming is done mostly in pools; *triathlon swimming* is done mainly in open water.
- Competitive swimmers have spent years gaining specialized skill and experience; more than 90 percent of *triathlon swimmers* are relatively unskilled and inexperienced in swimming, but still need to swim well now.
- Competitive swimming events are primarily 200 meters or less; *triathlon swimming* happens mainly at distances greater than 400 meters, often much greater.
- Competitive swimmers need to swim with intensity; *triathlon swimmers* need to swim effortlessly.
- Competitive swimmers can be specialists; *triathlon swimmers* have to train seriously in two other sports.

Triathlon swimming truly is a unique sport with unique challenges. This book focuses precisely on how to meet them, whether you are a first-timer seeking the confidence to tackle a long swim in open water, or an experienced competitor wanting to turn swimming into the best part of your triathlon.

The good news is that success at swimming for triathlon is far less dependent on "swimming talent" than you might imagine, and is actually within reach of every athlete. By mastering a finite set of easily learned skills, any smart and diligent athlete can swim dramatically better. I will guide you through that process in the pages to follow. By following this special Total Immersion *triathlon swimming* program, you'll learn to coach yourself so effectively that, within a short time, you will:

- Stand on shore at the beginning of any race and KNOW you can make the swim distance—and make it with ease.
- Know that you don't have to train as long or as hard in the pool as you thought.
- Know you really CAN master this sport that makes so many otherwise successful athletes feel unfit and uncoordinated.

Happy laps,

Terry Laughlin
New Paltz NY

Terry,

I just got your book, Swimming Made Easy, read it in one sitting and got so excited I dashed off to the pool. I have never spent better time in the water. The first couple of drills felt really awkward at first; I couldn't breath without using my arms to stabilize. Then the balance started to come. So I just merrily floated backwards and forwards for over an hour. For the first time in my life, I had a pretty good idea of how the body should feel in the water. At the end I just couldn't wait to start doing a bit of freestyle and was blown away. So this is what swimming is supposed to be like. Before my balance practice, I'd done 25 meters in 23 strokes and 35 seconds. Afterwards, I did it in 15 strokes and 28 seconds with much less effort. I couldn't believe it, I was just gliding and my arm movements felt as though they were almost incidental to what was going on. After one session I can imagine how much energy I'll have for the bike and run. YEAH!

Every triathlete should experience what TI swimming is like!!
Kind Regards
Craig Abrahamson—Sunshine Coast Australia

The lesson: As with any learning process, you'll have ups and downs, experience moments when you wonder if you're doing the right thing, if you really have the ability to improve your swimming. But the value of swimming in an examined way is that your body is a marvelous learning machine and it WILL learn new skills whenever you focus on swimming as a learning experience, instead of as a training regimen. So just get started and trust the value of immersing yourself in a learning experience.

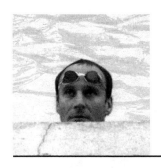

Part 1

Why Swimming Frustrates You and How You Can Achieve Fulfillment

Our first three chapters will give you a succinct explanation of

- Why you're not swimming as well as you'd like

- Why no amount of fitness, strength, or training will make any real difference

- Why swimming easier will improve your total tri-race time far more than swimming faster

By the time you move on to Chapter 4, you'll understand what constitutes good swimming and how you can embark on the path to Mastery just by changing the shape of your "vessel."

Chapter 1

True Confessions: If I'm So Fit, Why Is Swimming So Hard?

E very Saturday morning, somewhere in the USA (or Canada, the UK, Europe or Australia) 30 hopeful and somewhat apprehensive athletes, mostly triathletes and tri-wannabe's, gather in a classroom and talk about why they'd like to swim much better. It may sound like group therapy; but it's actually the orientation session of any Total Immersion weekend workshop. Some athletes confess that they can ride 60 miles or run 10 before breakfast yet gasp for breath after two laps in the pool. Others say they are tired of finding their bike standing alone when they finally stagger into the first transition — despite hour after hour of training laps in the pool.

Their frustration is simple and incredibly widespread. What is it about swimming that reduces otherwise fit and accomplished athletes to the point of needing TI "group therapy?" Why do all those tedious hours of repeats, laborious laps with kickboards, and wearying sessions with paddles and pull buoys never seem to produce improvement *or* yield results that are far too modest for the time and energy invested? Time on your feet and time in the seat work for running and biking. Why not for swimming?

The answer is that water is a completely different medium from air, and swimming is a completely unnatural activity for most land-based humans. In water, the rules are different. If you try to improve by swimming more and harder (an approach that comes naturally for cyclists or runners), you'll mainly make your "struggling skills" more permanent. If you seek instruction, you'll find that few coaches or teachers know how to teach you the skills and awareness that really make a difference. If you join a Masters swim team, your training program will be more organized than if you swim on your own, but unless you have the great fortune to be training with a coach who is just as good at teaching as training, you'll be a fitter flailer, but still not a *good* swimmer. Until you become a *good* swimmer, you'll always limit your potential as a triathlete. That's because you need to have a certain level of *efficiency* to get results from all your hours of training.

The solution is not elusive, costly, or time consuming. You *can* become a good enough swimmer to hugely improve your performance, potential, and fulfillment in triathlon. What it takes is a little knowledge and a willingness to *practice* swimming in a completely different way from how you *train* for the other two disciplines. Running and cycling are *sports*. Swimming — at least as you need to do it to be the best *triathlon swimmer* you can be — is an *art*. It's a movement art just as rigorous and exacting as gymnastics or martial arts. In order to succeed in it you need to do two things:

1. Become your own swimming coach.
2. Practice mindfully, patiently, and intelligently.

This book will give you the information and guidance to do both well.

Why Inefficient Swimming Is Limiting Your Triathlon Success

Success in triathlon obviously depends greatly on sheer fitness. Thus, 95 percent of your energy as a triathlete is usually devoted to maximizing your aerobic potential. Because you have to squeeze in three sports around work and family, you can't waste time on unproductive efforts. Yet until you become an efficient swimmer, you cannot realize the hard-won aerobic potential your training has earned you. Poor swimming not only puts you far back in the pack before you get to your strengths but also prevents you from spending your aerobic resources wisely and optimally. If you're a poor swimmer, you lack control over how hard you work in the water.

It's fairly simple to ration energy wisely while cycling and running. On the bike, you even have gears to help you maximize speed while minimizing effort. For a poor swimmer, there is no choice. For a large percentage of triathletes, simply making it through the swim is a survival test. If that's you, you have to flail and churn the whole time — an effort that doesn't earn you anything approximating a good swim time. It just allows you to finish wearily and far back in the pack.

Considering how little of the overall race distance and time swimming takes up, it consumes an extravagant amount of the energy available for the entire race. If you're like the great majority of triathletes, you aren't concerned solely about how slowly you swim. You probably worry more about how *hard* you work to swim that slowly. The most important message I give triathletes at Total Immersion workshops is this: **Your primary goal is not to swim faster.** Focus first on swimming *easier*, and let more speed be a natural product of your increased efficiency. You will improve your overall performance far more by saving energy for the bike and run than you will by swimming faster. But, better yet, as you become an efficient swimmer, you will *also* swim faster.

What It Takes to Be a Good Triathlon Swimmer

Unless you are an elite athlete, your smartest goal on the swim leg is to exit the water with a low heart rate. The swimming leg is too short for a speedier swim, by itself, to make a significant difference in a race that usually lasts for hours. If you do work hard enough to pick up a few minutes in the swim, that effort can easily cost you *many* minutes back on land. Conversely, many triathletes who have taken the TI workshop have found that their newfound efficiency, while it may have shaved just a few minutes off their swim time, resulted in *substantial* time drops for the rest of the race, simply because they were much fresher entering the first transition.

So your first goal as a *triathlon swimmer* is to gain the freedom to swim as easily as you wish — to be able to virtually float through a mile of swimming if you choose. To be able to choose how long or fast you stroke. And to be able to adjust both with the same ease with which you shift gears on your bike.

Your starting point for accomplishing these goals is to develop four foundation skills: balance, body alignment, body rotation, and coordinated propelling movements. The key is to have a relaxed, low-drag, fluent stroke at low speeds and to maintain all of those qualities as you move through your "swimming gears" to go faster. For most triathletes, swimming *speed* will probably never be essential (I'll explain the exceptions in a later chapter). Swimming *ease*, however, is a non-negotiable skill for every triathlete. Ease means efficiency, and efficiency leads to speed. And for those of you approaching the elite level, you must learn to swim fairly fast, without exerting yourself so much that you blow up on the run. And the same fundamentals that let the beginner acquire ease also let the more advanced athlete develop efficient "gearing" for swimming faster when necessary.

Your essential goal as a triathlete is to have more control when swimming — more ability to decide how hard to work, how much stroke length and stroke rate to use at any moment, and the skill to find the most efficient way to go faster when needed. Let's begin learning how to gain that control and why, as a triathlete, you have plenty of company in figuring out The Swimming Puzzle.

Chapter 2

Two-Dollar Gas: The Secret of Economy

Whenever the price of gasoline nears $2.00 per gallon, SUVs and other gas-guzzlers lose a bit of their popularity, while car pooling and public transportation gain ground. I drive a gas-sipping Saab, but my response is to drive with a lighter foot, avoid nonessential trips, and combine errands. As a triathlete, your training time and energy are two-dollar gasoline and there's no strategic fuel reserve to lessen the cost. Triathlon is a demanding discipline. Most triathletes cannot make a full-time job of training; thus, economy is the smartest success strategy of all.

By *economy* I mean: (1) efficient use of your limited training time and (2) efficient use of your body so that your available energy goes into forward motion and not struggle. If you take to heart the lessons of this book, you'll need to spend less time in the pool...and will accomplish *more* than in your current program. If you get excited about shaving *minutes* off your bike time with an expensive set of wheels, think how you'll feel if you spend almost nothing to learn how to swim with such ease that you might cut an *hour* or more from your total Ironman time (as has happened to more than one Total Immersion alum).

Your constant goal as a multi-sport athlete is to develop the capacity to go farther and faster and, more important (because most triathletes are in their 30s or older), the capability to do both without breaking down.

Faster race times are the motivation for training. Therefore you need to be rigorous in spending your precious training time wisely so that it brings *clear benefits to race time*. Training simply to prove that you can endure prodigious workloads would make sense if places were awarded to those with the most impressive logbook. But most triathletes have job and family responsibilities, and the best training program is one that produces the fastest race times with the least time and effort. And, as you'll learn, training intelligently is even more critical in swimming than in the other two disciplines.

Economy

In the physiology lab, economy is measured by how much oxygen you use while exercising, because oxygen consumption is the best indicator of how much muscle fuel you burn to go a given distance at a given speed. In the pool or on the road, heart rate is the most practical marker for economy because it helps trained athletes develop an acute sense of how hard they are working at any given moment. If a competitive swimmer spends fewer heartbeats (i.e., consumes less oxygen or fuel) to do the same work — let's say, to swim 100 meters in 1 minute, 20 seconds—she has two choices for how to use the energy surplus she's created. Sprinters can swim the distance faster, perhaps improving their 100-meter time to 1 minute and 15 seconds. Longer-distance swimmers can choose to maintain the same speed for longer, swimming 200 meters in 2 minutes, 40 seconds, or 400 meters in 5 minutes, 20 seconds. And perhaps ultimately 1500 meters in 20 minutes. *Tri-swimmers* have a third option — for most the smartest one — to save much of that surplus for cycling and/or running.

The longer the race, the more important economy becomes. When swimming a short distance — 50 to 100 meters — you could conceivably muscle your way through it. But there is no sprint distance in *tri-swimming*. Even a "sprint" triathlon starts with a 400-meter swim, which is a long way to be wasting energy. And the 2.4-mile Ironman swim is 250 percent farther than any Olympic swimming event. The opportunity to waste energy — to misspend heartbeats you badly need to bike 112 miles and run a marathon — is astronomical. And as we have heard countless times from

TI workshop alumni who have chosen to apply most of what they learned from us to swimming easier, rather than faster while their times for the swim leg have indeed improved markedly, their race splits in cycling and running have also improved dramatically, because they "save heartbeats" in the water for use on land.

From a *tri-swimming* perspective, in this book I'll show you how to

1. *Drive with a lighter foot* (swim with a lower HR and energy cost).
2. *Avoid unnecessary trips* (get more benefit from fewer and easier swim-training laps).
3. *Acquire a "smart" car* (retool your stroke for efficiency).

The effect of all three will be to turn the "cost of fuel" — your time and energy — back to those halcyon days of 30-cent gas.

Chapter 3

How to Start Swimming Better Immediately

Perhaps you didn't start out thinking "I'd like to be a swimmer," but as soon as you mailed your first triathlon entry, swimming became a necessary evil. Or as most triathletes perceive it: "something I have to endure in order to do the two other sports I find much easier and more satisfying." And you probably began by applying what you had learned from cycling or running: *mileage equals improvement.* You may even have seen some modest progress in the beginning. But if you're like 98 percent of triathletes I've met, you soon reached a state one described as "Terminal mediocrity: no matter how much I swim, I never get any better." There's a logical reason for that. Unlike running or cycling, which you probably did reasonably well from age 7, with little instruction or "practice," swimming well requires lots of both. Thousands of athletes who can run or bike long distances with ease, find themselves exhausted after a few laps of swimming. They know they're in shape, but swimming seems to require its own special kind of fitness. So they do yet more laps, hoping it will come. But if you're an unskilled swimmer, all those laps do is make your "struggling skills" more enduring. No matter how many laps you do, you'll never have enough fitness to compensate for the energy you waste.

This is why triathletes have responded enthusiastically to the simple logic of Total Immersion. We explain your difficulties in a way that makes sense. We suggest simple approaches that even inexperienced swimmers can confidently practice in a way that they *know* will make a difference. And, finally, we've replaced boring workouts with purposeful and interesting practice. The result is a style of swimming that, among its many virtues, *always feels good*. It looks good, too. TI swimmers are instantly recognizable to other swimmers by their unusual flow and ease.

The Water Is Your Swimming Problem

The reason you're not swimming as well as you'd like is *because you're a land animal in water*. Humans are "hard-wired" to fight the water rather than work *with* it. There are literally only a few dozen people on the planet who have almost totally solved this. Swimmers such as Ian Thorpe (and former Olympic medallists such as Sheila Taormina) have learned to overcome the "human-swimming problem" because: a) they're gifted with a rare sense of *how to be one with the water* (coaches call this "feel of the water") and b) they've spent millions of yards (typically guided more by that intuition than by their coaches) developing a preternatural grace and economy.

You, on the other hand — along with virtually everyone else on the planet — probably swim more like "Eric the Eel," the athlete from Equatorial Guinea who won our hearts and admiration at the Sydney games for finishing the 100-meter freestyle, despite the fact that every stroke seemed like agonizing struggle for him. *Human swimming* looks like this mainly because water is an unnatural, even threatening, environment. Our bodies were not designed to travel easily through it, and our basic instincts as land-based animals cause us to fight it, not work *with* it. Our discomfort creates tension; we respond with turbulent churning. Both keep us from moving freely and fluently. Since water is a fluid, flowing freely through it is essential to efficiency. Any swimmer can learn how to do this. The first step is to understand what's holding you back.

Three Mistakes Every "Human Swimmer" Makes:

Chances are, you've thought there was something wrong with you because:

1.   You think you'll sink. Fighting "that sinking feeling" is something all humans do from their very first stroke. After a very few additional strokes, the struggle to stay afloat becomes a habit. The result? Most of your energy and too much of what you hope are propelling actions (i.e., your pull and kick) are spent keeping you from sinking, instead of acting to move you forward.

2.   You try to overpower the water. Water is 800 times denser than air. In essence, it's a wall. If air can feel so resistant at 20 miles an hour on a bicycle, then imagine how much resistance the water throws at you at even the slowest speeds. As you get a little faster — particularly if your legs tend to sink as you swim, drag goes up to almost inconceivable levels. Want to better understand how that wall of water reacts to your body? Next time you go to the pool, try walking half a lap. What you feel is drag. Next, try running the same distance. Ouch! And how do we instinctively respond to resistance? Mainly by pushing harder. But all that does is increase drag still more.

3.   You churn your arms. The medium that was too solid when you tried to walk through it suddenly becomes very elusive when you look for a handhold to support or propel yourself.

When you try to push on it, it just swirls away. Compared with running, in which we move through thin air and propel by pushing off solid ground, swimming is like running through a Jello swamp. And because the water offers neither support nor traction, our natural response is turbulent churning, like wheels spinning on ice. This increases energy cost and the extra turbulence increases drag. A double whammy.

The 5-Step Swimming Solution

The reason TI methods create such fast transformation is simple: They've had to. By teaching hundreds of workshops that last just a weekend — rather than lessons that go on for weeks — by having *hours* to teach fluency, not months or years as most coaches do, we've learned to eliminate wasted steps. And since many of our students are inexperienced, we've done away with all of the technical mumbo-jumbo. Our instruction is simple and clear. And virtually everyone who follows five basic, but non-negotiable, steps learns to swim better with almost ridiculous ease.

*Do nothing more difficult until you've
learned to be effortlessly horizontal.*

1. Learn balance. Balance — the feeling that you are effortlessly supported by the water and free to devote all of your efforts to efficient propulsion — is what makes Ian Thorpe and other Olympians swim as beautifully as they do. Lack of balance — the sense that you must constantly fight that sinking feeling — is what made Eric the Eel swim as he did. In the TI program, mastery of balance is the non-negotiable first step: You do nothing more difficult until you have learned to be effortlessly horizontal and completely supported in a few basic positions. And you continue practicing these positions until balance feels completely natural. When you learn balance first, you not only stop fighting the water and wasting energy, you also learn comfort and ease, which allows you to master every other swimming skill much faster...and ultimately will let you virtually glide through a triathlon swim of any distance.

2. Unlearn struggle; learn harmony. Being able to relax and enjoy the support of the water is just the starting point of a series of sequenced movement skills. At every step, it's critical to remember that your human DNA, combined with your history of "practicing struggle," makes you incredibly vulnerable to regressing. The great advantage of the TI process is that it starts with simple movements and positions and progresses in small steps. At every step, you have the opportunity to eliminate struggle and let fluency replace it as a habit. When you master basic balance, and move on to active balance and beyond, remember that the qualities of fluent movement you will be practicing are just as important as the mechanics of drills and skills.

3. Learn to roll effortlessly. *Human swimming* propulsion instinctively starts with arm-and-leg-churning. What that does best is make waves and create turbulence. Fish propel by undulating their bodies. Scientists have yet to puzzle out how, with little "horsepower" and resisted by drag, fish can reach speeds of 50 mph and beyond, without ever seeming to *try*. That effortless power is produced by core-based propulsion. You'll learn to tap effortless power when your rhythms and movements originate in your core body, not in your arms and legs. Those core-body rhythms release the energy and power that subsequently become a strong, economical swimming stroke. You learn them by advancing from static to active (rolling) balance drills.

4. Learn to *pierce* the water. Torpedoes, submarines, and racing boats are sleekly shaped for the same reason fish are: to avoid drag. Because drag increases exponentially as speed goes up (twice the speed equals *four* times the drag), drag reduction pays off exponentially as you swim faster. That's why humans who learn to slip through the smallest possible hole in the water see such rapid and dramatic improvement. Slippery swimmers need far less power or effort to swim at any speed. Awareness of slipping through the smallest possible hole in the water is maintained at every step of our skill-building sequence.

5. Learn fluent, coordinated propelling movements. To most swimmers, technique means "how you use your hands to push water toward your feet." That's the starting point and remains the primary focus of conventional instruction and stroke drills. In the TI approach, arm stroking is among the *last* things we teach: First, you acquire a long, balanced, needle-shaped, and effortlessly rotating core body. Then you link your pull and kick to the body's movements and rhythms. As your propelling actions, practiced first in "switch" drills, gradually grow into "strokes," we maintain a focus on keeping them coordinated and integrated with core-body rhythm. Our slogan is "swim with your body, not your arms and legs." And the moment your speed, effort, or fatigue causes you to feel "disconnected," it's time to slow down and regain your flow. Never... ever... "practice struggle."

But remember: None of these positions or skills is natural or instinctive. You must apply yourself to learning them. The clear and logical course of instruction in the chapters that follow should put you on the path to better swimming immediately. But first I'll ask you to forget everything you "know" about swimming so you can learn a completely fresh way to move through the water, a way I guarantee will make more sense, feel better and make improvement easier than anything you've tried before.

Dear Terry,

Early last year I started competing in sprint triathlons. I trained my proverbials off to become physically the fittest I have ever been, but remain a dreadful swimmer. Fortunately I came across your web site and purchased your book and video. Where I have been going wrong is so clearly described in the book that I instantly felt optimistic for the first time that I could actually start to enjoy swimming instead of dreading it and, perhaps, make some gains in my competition times.

I'm only 3 weeks into practice working on hand-lead drills but already feel so much more relaxed and controlled; all that arm/neck pressure I used to exert to get my head out of the water to breathe has disappeared since I learned how to balance and rotate my core. I can't wait to attend a workshop in the UK. For now, however, I thank you sincerely for your work; it's revelational stuff!

Cameron Irving
Huddersfield
West Yorkshire
England.

The lesson: As soon as you have correctly identified your swimming problem and started working on a clear and logical path to solutions, your sense of your future prospects will brighten immediately.

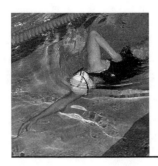

Part 2

The Smart Swimming Solution

In the next six chapters, we'll explain the smartest way to become a more effective swimmer. The information we'll present is simple, readily available, and logical...but widely ignored by swimmers and triathletes, who choose the much harder, more frustrating route of generic training. But not you. In the next few pages, you'll learn the most clever and reliable way to improve your swimming, and you'll gain all the tools you need to train smarter and more efficiently than virtually every swimmer on earth.

Chapter 4

Stroke Length: How You Can Swim Like Ian Thorpe

While special oxygen-analyzing equipment may be needed to measure economy in the research lab, in the pool economy is easy to recognize. The pool where I train is filled with thoroughly "average" swimmers. Their splashy, choppy, noisy strokes are the norm. The pool at Auburn University, where we did a TI team workshop for the school's two-time NCAA Championship team, is filled with extraordinary swimmers. Wherever we looked — even before we began teaching — almost all of the fifty men and women swimmers were practicing long, relaxed, unhurried strokes, with little noise or splash and a marked absence of visible effort.

Good swimmers have one thing in common: They make it look easy. Genuinely great swimmers — there are only a few dozen in the entire world — are so fishlike that they look downright elegant. The latest example is 2000 Olympic champion Ian Thorpe, who shattered world records in Sydney, while taking what The New York Times described as "strokes of languid purpose."

Since 1992, Alexander Popov had been my favorite exemplar of swimming economy. While Popov, for 10 years the World's Fastest Human, is enormously gifted, he and his coach also made a purposeful decade-long effort to emphasize the practice of fluidity and control at all speeds. The impression I get from champions such as Thorpe and Popov is that they always seem to be *of* the water, not just *in* it. The word that best captures the quality of their swimming is *flow*.

And what is the secret to flow? For years I was convinced it was pure talent: great swimmers somehow knew *in their bones* how to remain fluid and smooth when going fast. The rest of us could just watch in envy. But ten years of intensive teaching have shown me that "Fishlike" swimming is possible for anyone who pursues it logically and patiently. At every Total Immersion workshop, we start on Saturday morning with splashy, choppy, "average" swimmers, like those that fill my pool, and yours. By Sunday afternoon, the flow pattern right across the pool is much like what we saw at Auburn.

Using simple information, you too can understand exactly how to achieve flow and then, to a surprising degree, achieve it for yourself. Once you've "broken the code" of fluid, relaxed swimming, you can consciously practice, as Alex Popov does, the movements and qualities that produce it, and that all but guarantee you'll swim your best. I won't promise you'll swim as fast as an Olympian, but you *will* swim as well as *you're* capable of swimming.

The key to being the best swimmer you can be is a longer stroke or, as swim pros call it, Stroke Length. This "secret" is actually widely known, but almost perversely ignored, by coaches and swimmers, who continue to pursue success mainly through sheer sweat, even though more and harder laps actually tend to make your stroke shorter, not longer. Hard work, without sufficient care and thought, will actually *slow* most swimmers' progress.

An even more powerful impediment than habit is instinct. Most every swimmer who wants to go faster automatically thinks first of churning the arms faster. And a faster stroke (i.e., higher stroke rate, or SR) results in a *shorter* stroke — again, just the ticket for swimming slower, instead.

Stroke Length: The Mark of Champions

How do we know stroke length is so important? Since 1976, more than a dozen researchers have analyzed the results of meets at all levels, from high-school championships to the Olympics, to figure out what made the

faster swimmers faster. Each study produced the same result: Winners took fewer strokes. Test it yourself at any local pool or at your next workout: Count strokes per length for slower swimmers and compare with faster swimmers. The faster swimmers will almost certainly take fewer strokes.

This simple insight has incredible potential to transform your own swimming, if you'll just use it. But as I said, most swimmers or triathletes continue to train as if the pace clock and yardage total were all that mattered. If even one study had identified aerobic power as the key to better swimming, such overwhelming focus on distance, time, and effort would make more sense. But none did. Likewise, plenty of athletes pump iron or muscle their way through endless laps with huge paddles and/or drag suits, as if sheer power was the way to swim faster. Yet when scientists study the impact of power on performance, they usually find the best swimmers in the world are *less* powerful than any number of mediocre swimmers. So weight-room visits and power-oriented swim sets aren't the answer either.

None of this is to suggest that fitness is unimportant. But at the Olympics, *everyone* has worked hard; *everyone* is incredibly fit. Yet certain swimmers still have an edge over all the others. And that edge, up to 90 percent of the time, is a longer stroke.

What, Exactly, *Is* Stroke Length?

You can work more effectively on your Stroke Length (for simplicity, I'll refer to it as SL, and to stroke *count* per length of the pool as spl), if you understand it, but SL is one of the most poorly understood terms in swimming. Even though swimmers are beginning to grasp that a long stroke is advantageous, most are still unsure of exactly what SL means or how to make a stroke longer. They mostly think of SL as "how far you reach forward and push back."

Coaches usually recognize that there's more to SL than just "the length of your stroke," but few understand how to significantly improve it. When I eavesdrop at workouts, I hear directives such as, "You've got to make your stroke longer!" which the swimmer naturally interprets as "Reach forward and push back more." This will produce a small increase in SL, but 99.9% of the time that increase will be lost the moment the

swimmer tries to go faster. Nor will it bring the swimmer anywhere near his or her best possible SL. So the swimmer remains unconvinced and goes back to relying on SR (stroke rate) for speed.

For years, I struggled to increase my own SL without much success. So long as I worked on it by trying to push more water back, I managed to shave about one stroke from my average each year or two. Then my teaching experiences began showing me the importance of being balanced and slippery, and all at once I was able to lop off a jaw-dropping three SPL in a few weeks — and to help other swimmers score SL improvements of up to 50% literally overnight. Often, these were people who understood the value of SL and had been trying for years to improve it.

The reason stroke length doesn't have a lot to do with arm length, or with how you push water back, is SL is *how far your body travels each time you take a stroke*, and your success in minimizing drag influences it far more than how you stroke. You'll learn how to minimize drag in the next three chapters.

Run Like a Greyhound; Swim Like a Fish

The key to becoming a better swimmer can be found in a simple equation:

$$V = SL \times SR$$

Velocity equals Stroke Length multiplied by Stroke Rate.

Count strokes regularly and begin improving immediately.

How fast you swim (V) is a product of how far you travel on each stroke (SL), multiplied by how fast you take those strokes (SR). In that way, at least, swimming is no different from running or in-line skating or cross-country skiing, where SL and SR refer to Stride Length and Stride Rate.

SL is as important in swimming as in running or cross-country skiing.

Throughout the animal kingdom, the really fast creatures — race horses, greyhounds, cheetahs, Marion Jones, Michael Johnson — use about the same stride rate at all speeds. They run faster by taking *longer* strides, not by taking them faster. (Please note though that elite runners and triathletes have higher stride rates than recreational runners and make subtle changes in speed by tweaking their stride rate while maintaining a biomechanically efficient stride length.) Using real numbers, a runner doubling his speed from a 10-minute-per-mile pace to 5-minute miles, might well do it by stretching each stride from 18 to 33 inches (an 83% increase), while increasing stride rate by only 8%, from 83 to 90 per minute. But in the water, for all the reasons I explained earlier, we humans do just the opposite, resorting to churning our arms madly when we want more speed.

It seems self-evident that a longer stroke or stride would be more effi-cient than a shorter one, but in the water a longer stroke is *much* more efficient. Here's why. First, there's the energy cost of a higher SR. As you increase SR, the energy cost goes up by a *cube* of that increase. Double your stroke rate and you burn energy eight (2 x 2 x 2) times faster. Second, there's the effect of a higher SR on coordination. As SR (and your heart rate) increases, your ability to stay coordinated and fluent diminish-es dramatically. As your form becomes increasingly ragged and inefficient, energy cost goes up even more. And, finally, you disturb the water around you far more when you're churning than when stroking smoothly. A fast turnover is like swimming in white water. Not only is drag higher in tur-bulent water, but also your hands can't "grip" churned-up water nearly so well as they grip still water. One of the surest ways to find still water to pull is to swim with a greater SL and lower SR.

Learn to be slippery and to "pierce"
the water, even when sighting.

How Can I Improve My SL?

As soon as you begin counting strokes, you'll recognize that virtually every choice you make in training influences your SL in some way — the dis-tance of your repeats, how much you rest between them, the length of your sets, how fast you swim, your heart rate. But the single most important reason for a mediocre SL is *failure to pay attention to it*. If you are not consciously monitoring how your SL holds up at various speeds and distances (by counting strokes), your instincts will drag you back into too much reliance on SR. In fact, if you were to put this book away now and do nothing more ambitious than count your strokes regularly and set some personal standards or an acceptable upper limit, you would immediately start improving. When you do monitor your count, you'll be alerted as soon as your SL falls too steeply and can immediately take steps to fix it. And what might those steps be?

SL can be improved in two ways. The easiest way is to minimize drag, and you do this by simply *repositioning* your body in the water to make yourself *more slippery*. We'll help you do that by showing you how to *pierce* the water. The more slippery your body line, the farther you will travel, with more ease and less deceleration, on a given amount of propulsion. The second way to improve SL is to maximize propulsion, and you do this by focusing on doing a better job of *moving your body forward*. To improve that, we'll show you how to replace exhausting arm churning with coordinated whole-body movements.

When I began teaching TI workshops in 1989, I had recently become acquainted with an independent thinker named Bill Boomer who urged coaches to at least pay *some* attention to "vessel-shaping." I decided to balance my attention between showing people how to propel themselves better and teaching them how to be more slippery, which in 1989 was a highly experimental art. I was clear on one thing: I would measure my success as a teacher by how much my students improved their SL.

And, from the start, I noticed a striking phenomenon. When I was successful in teaching swimmers to *stroke* better, I would see a modest improvement in their SL. When I was successful in teaching them to *pierce the water*, I would see *dramatic* improvement. Norton Davey, one of the few 70+ athletes to complete an Ironman, was a prime example. At a TI workshop in Chicago in 1994, it took him 36 strokes to swim 25 yards as we videotaped him on Saturday morning. By Sunday afternoon he had increased his SL by 100%, taking only 18 strokes, but the pushing-water part of his stroke, as shown on underwater video, was virtually unchanged. His body position, though, had changed from about a 30-degree "uphill" posture on Saturday to very nearly horizontal on Sunday. Countless experiences such as that got my attention in a hurry, and we soon began to devote more and more of our limited teaching time to "slippery swimming."

How Many Strokes Should I Take?

The simplest way to monitor your SL is to make a habit of counting your strokes, at all speeds, and on virtually every length. That will give you a basis for evaluating whether you're spending your precious pool time concentrating on things that will really help you swim faster or more easily. You'll find there's not a single number that represents your "best" stroke count. You'll have a stroke count *range* — fewer on shorter repeats and/or when you're swimming slower; more when you're going farther or faster.

Your primary goals should be to:

1) gradually lower that range;

2) reduce the difference between its top and bottom; and

3) do the majority of your training in the lower half of your range. If your range was 17 to 24 SPL last year and 14 to 20 this year (or if you can swim faster at each point in that 17-to-24 range), stay the course; you're doing something right.

But at what point have you gone far enough? Now and again, we'll see a workshop pupil proudly swim for the video camera on Saturday morning in a very low count, perhaps 12 strokes, because they've read my first book and taken its message to heart, working unswervingly to shave strokes. But their 12-stroke lap is anything but efficient. It's typically lurching and non-rhythmic, and there's a whole lot of kicking going on.

I'll take the blame for that, having failed in that book to make clear that the goal of our instruction is to help you reach your *optimal*, not maximal SL. We don't want you straining to reach the lowest count you can squeeze out. We want you to free yourself to swim at an efficient count that you can maintain with relatively little effort, and relatively little kicking. These swimmers would actually have been better off with a relaxed and rhythmic 15 strokes than the 12 they were straining to hold.

The key to that freedom, ease, and control is balance, the one skill of swimming that is non-negotiable...but also incredibly rare. Let's get straight to it.

Chapter 5

Balance: Becoming Fishlike Starts Here

I f there's one moment at every TI workshop that can be
described as an epiphany, it's when our students first realize
they can float — feel effortlessly supported by the water — just
by changing their body position. For most, this is a total revelation —
so accustomed are they to fighting "that sinking feeling" with every
stroke. That sensation, created by a drill so simple that 90 percent of
our students master it in 10 minutes, is so transforming that one of our
alums exulted in an e-mail to me, "I've been swimming twice a day
since the workshop because I'm afraid if I wait too long I'll have forgotten how it feels to be balanced. Every time I get in I pray, 'please,
please, feel like it did last time.' I've never felt anything like it; I'm
literally just floating along!"

That sense of ease and comfort is transforming for swimmers who
have struggled for years without *ever* feeling good. Ten minutes, and one
simple skill, have made them feel more capable than anything else in their
swimming experience. That's why mastering balance is the non-negotiable foundation of "fishlike" swimming — the skill that must be learned
by every would-be swimmer before attempting *anything* more advanced.

Which simply means that learning to swim is no different from learning
to walk or learning any other land-based skill. Many years ago, just learning
to stand unaided, and then take a few shaky steps, took each of us weeks of

utterly concentrated effort. But it was essential to every movement skill that
followed, from basic play skills such as running and bicycling to advanced
athletic skills such as gymnastics, dance, or downhill skiing.

In each instance the body's center of gravity (several inches below
the navel) must be kept artfully aligned over the feet while the body is
moving in ways likely to upset that alignment. We spend virtually every
waking minute consciously or unconsciously practicing dynamic balance
in that way. And our motivation to excel at it is great for, if we don't, we'll
be terrible at sports — and be much more likely to fall and fracture things.

Part of the reason it has taken so long for swimmers and coaches to
understand how essential it is to master balance is that being unbalanced
doesn't have so serious a penalty in the water as on land. Rather than a
painful fall and instant lesson, we start doing laps any way we can and simply get tired from all the extra drag of a body moving towards its natural
(i.e., vertical) position (and begin learning how to struggle). Our reaction
to that is "I need to get in better shape."

Ten years of teaching have shown us that *every* swimmer who has not
consciously worked on balance has room to improve on it. Even Olympic
swimmers have told me they could feel their hips become lighter and higher after practicing simple balance drills, though we could not always *see* a
striking difference. But with Olympic medals won by the tiniest of margins,
even fractional improvements in efficiency loom large.

The immediate improvement in *every* swimmer to whom we've
taught our basic balance drills has shaped TI methods as nothing else has.
It's also shaped the thinking of hundreds of coaches who have attended a
TI workshop and seen how rapidly a sense of balance can transform a
struggling swimmer into a fluent one. Mastering balance is not only important in its own right, but also impacts every part of the stroke. Here's how.

1. *Balance keeps you horizontal and slippery.* Imagine kicking
with a board angled slightly upward. The increased drag would make kicking a *lot* harder. Now imagine how much drag your whole body can create
when positioned at a similar angle. If you're not perfectly horizontal, it's a
lot more work to move yourself forward than if you are horizontal. After
viewing underwater video of thousands of swimmers, we've concluded that

well over 90% have room to improve their balance, including many who appear from the deck to be doing fine.

Usually the best-hidden imbalance is that which happens only momentarily during the stroke (e.g., while breathing in freestyle). Viewed in slow-motion or stop-action from under water, it shows up glaringly. The swimmer usually has no idea this is going on at all *until* he or she begins regular balance practice and realizes how much better it feels to be completely supported by the water.

2. Balance saves you from wasting energy fighting "that sinking feeling." Let's clear up one thing right now: Your body is *supposed* to sink. Huge amounts of energy are wasted because of the nearly universal misunderstanding that good body position means riding high in the water.

Novice swimmers spend upwards of 90 percent of their energy just trying to keep from sinking. Their "survival stroke" leaves little energy for moving forward. More accomplished swimmers — no longer in any danger of drowning — waste energy, too, because they've heard that good swimmers ride high on the water. Coaches sagely repeat it, and swimmers grimly try to do it. The reality? A speedboat will not hydroplane until it's reached at least 33 mph, and no human swimmer has ever exceeded 5 mph. The pointless effort to stay on top not only squanders energy, but also keeps your arms and legs so busy pressing down (to keep you up) that they have no opportunity to propel you *forward*.

You save much more energy by *learning to sink in a horizontal position* instead of fighting to stay on top. As soon as you learn to find an effortlessly horizontal position in the water, you eliminate needless tension, you gain flow and ease, and you save energy for propulsion.

3. Balance "liberates your limbs" to propel more efficiently. Coaches often observe a dropped elbow or splayed-leg and order, "Keep those elbows up!" or "Keep your legs closer!" They're really asking the swimmer to correct the symptom, like a doctor ordering you to "Get that temperature down!" rather than seeking the cause of your fever.

Swimmers have an instinctive understanding that it's better to remain horizontal and stable. When they sense imbalance, they instinctively use their arms or legs to fix it. These compensating or stabilizing actions appear to the coach as stroke errors. But when the underlying imbalance is corrected, many of the more visible errors often disappear. The arms are freed to perform their most valuable function — lengthening the bodyline and holding on to the water. The legs are freer to stay effortlessly in sync with core-body rotation. The stroke automatically becomes far more efficient.

4. Balance frees more of your power. A baseball slugger's power is useless if he swings from an off-balance stance. An in-line skater, cross-country skier, or speed skater's powerful quads can do little good if the rest of the body isn't stable and positioned for the push. No good athlete attempts to perform in anything other than full dynamic balance. On land, grounded by gravity and needing *all* of your body's power to excel, your body just knows it can't deliver if it's not balanced.

In the water, it's different. Supported by buoyancy, your body weight is only 10% of what it is on land. And because you're not on solid ground, you're similarly restricted from using all of your potential power. On top of that, without those clear dry-land signals, your body's balancing instincts can't tell you how you're limiting the power you *do* have.

But limiting it you are, because swimming power comes from core-body rotation, which triggers the *kinetic chain*, which powers the arms and legs. As we've seen in thousands of unbalanced swimmers on underwater video, a swimmer who lacks dynamic balance loses the ability to rotate freely. Many of these swimmers, aware that something is holding them back, spend hour after hour doing lat pulls and tricep presses. Truth is, they already have ample power and could tap it instantly by improving their balance.

5. Balance frees you to be more fluent. The unbalanced swimmer, especially in freestyle, is often trapped in a cycle of frantic movement. He responds to the feeling of sinking by churning his arms more. The faster he churns, the shorter his strokes become, and the more strokes he has to take to maintain speed. Eventually, he's flailing his arms frantically just to keep moving.

As soon as you master balance, you escape the trap. You can move at the same speed with a far more leisurely stroke, can find a more natural and fluent body rhythm, and will swim in calmer water.

Getting Your Balance

We define balance as being "effortlessly horizontal" in the water. The key word is *effortless*. It's possible to achieve a horizontal position if you do things such as kick hard, skip breaths or use your arms for support. But we're after horizontal balance with minimal kicking, breathing at will, and with "weightless" arms. And this kind of effortless balance is achieved by creatively *repositioning* your body parts and redistributing your body mass. You can almost forget about pulling and kicking.

The way to do it is fairly simple. First, keep your head in a natural, neutral position — as close as possible to the way you hold it when you're *not* swimming. Second, shift your body weight forward. "Press your buoy," as I call the process of pushing your normally buoyant chest cavity into the water, until you feel the water pushing you back out. Pressing in, rather than trying to stay on top, is, of course, counterintuitive. But virtually everything about water balance is non-instinctive, as TI Senior Coach Emmett Hines explains.

"For a child learning to balance while walking, a certain amount of time and repetition are needed. Moreover, that repetition needs to be pretty much just walking."

"Now for a person to maintain balance while break-dancing on a trotting horse's back (I took my kid to the circus last week), to avoid falling off and getting trampled by the elephant next in line, a great deal more time and repetition are needed. And that repetition needs to be pretty much just break-dancing on a horse's back, or pieces of that skill ordered in a progressive manner, so as to end up with something people will pay to see."

"My sense is that swimming is more like break-dancing on a horse's back than walking. Whenever we do anything in the water, the neuromuscular system is inextricably drawn to the 'wrong' conclusions about what balance is and how to achieve it. Not wrong for land-based activity — wrong for water-based activity."

Which suggests that it takes a fairly deliberate and exacting process to master this elusive skill. Here are the elements.

Balancing Your Freestyle
"Hide" Your Head

If you've read my first TI book, you know I stressed the importance of leaning on your chest or "buoy." That's still important, but additional years of teaching swimmers balance have shown us that head position is actually more essential than pressing your buoy. In fact, simply getting the head in a neutral (aligned-with-the-spine) position eliminates about 70% of the balance problems for students in our workshops. So our teaching progression now starts with teaching swimmers to "hide" the head. Once that's accomplished, we show them how to "press the buoy."

From the deck, it looks like this: Our coaches know your head is in the right position when we can see no more than a sliver of the back of your head or cap above the surface any time you're looking down. From your point of view, it should feel as if:

- a thin film of water could flow over the back of your head at any time
- you're looking directly at the bottom between breaths, using peripheral vision to peek just a bit forward
- you're leading with the top of your head, rather than with your nose
- your hips and legs feel much lighter and are riding noticeably higher

Hiding your head does not mean burying it, nor pressing it down. It simply means holding your head in a neutral position, the way you hold it when you're not swimming. When I'm coaching, as I look across the pool, I want to see that tiny sliver of the back of your head showing above the surface whenever you're not breathing. Or a thin film of water flowing over it. Ask a friend to watch you as you swim and drill, after showing them the photo on the next page.

Ask a friend if your head position looks like this.

Swim "Downhill"

We may no longer emphasize this as much as previously, but for many people — and particularly triathletes who are quite lean or have weak kicks or rigid ankles (from years of running) — consciously shifting weight forward, constantly leaning on your chest, remains very helpful. Hiding your head should make your balance much better, but if you still feel your hips and legs sinking, then lean on your chest too. How much? Press in until you feel the water pushing you back out. Press in until you feel as if your hips are light, as if the water is simply carrying you. When that happens, you're experiencing the sensation we call "swimming downhill." You're not really, but the contrast with your prior ordeal swimming uphill will have you imploring "please, please feel like this every time." Continue doing it very consciously until it starts to happen naturally. If you're one of the confirmed "sinkers," this could take as much as six months of patient effort.

Reach with a "Weightless" Arm

The best indicator that you are a truly balanced freestyler is the sensation of having a "weightless" arm. With poor balance, or a high head position, you have to use your arms to try to keep from sinking. The weight of your head and body drives them down as you try to reach forward. A balanced swimmer should be able to feel as if the extending arm is weightless, just floating effortlessly — almost leisurely — forward, until you choose to make your catch and begin stroking.

Drill with Total Patience

The most important advice I give to the 20% of workshop attendees who are "balance challenged" is to do as little swimming as possible. Until you have at least the basics of balance, you will almost certainly "practice struggle" to an unacceptable degree while doing whole-stroke swimming. It is essential to take all the time necessary to patiently move through the basic balance drills until effortless support begins to feel natural. Don't swim and don't even do much advanced drilling. Just stay with the most basic drills — Lesson One in the drill section that begins on page 75 — almost to the exclusion of everything else.

Use the fistglove® stroke trainer

After mastering Lessons 1 through 3 (see pages 75 to 98), one of the simplest and quickest ways to further develop your basic balance skills, while doing "switch" drills and whole-stroke swimming, is to wear fist-glove® stroke trainers for 50 percent or more of your pool time. These black latex "mittens" tightly wrap your hand into a fist and make it impossible to use your arm as a support lever or to muscle your way through the water. They force you to use your torso for balance and support and encourage you to use much more finesse while swimming. Soon, a weightless arm is your only option. For more information on fistgloves®, visit www.totalimmersion.net and read Chapter 9.

Should I Use a Pull Buoy?

Ordinarily my answer would be no. Once a swimmer has learned balance, I'd say he should never use a pull buoy again; a balanced body is its own perfect buoy. But for the 10% of swimmers with the most stubborn balance challenge, there may be some benefit in doing a limited amount of pull-buoy practice. The basic problem with pull buoys is they provide artificial balance; take the buoy off and it's lost. If, however, you wear it just long enough to sharpen your kinesthetic sense of how it feels to have your hips and legs effortlessly supported and how that can free your arms to simply glide forward (see weightless arm above), you can try to replicate the sensation without the buoy. You might spend 7 to 10 minutes alternating one length with the buoy, two without, mindfully trying to make the buoy-free laps feel progressively more like the buoy-supported laps.

If you typically swim with a frantic kick (not unusual for runners), you might also benefit from spending part of your practice time with a pull buoy. Again, use it to learn what it feels like to have your hips and legs feel effortlessly supported so that you don't need to use them to stay afloat.

What about My Wetsuit?

Wetsuits are universally popular with triathletes for one primary reason. They instantly solve the balance problem. Yes, they help keep you warm in cold water but, more important, they make you comfortable and confident. In Chapter 20, I'll give detailed guidance on how to use that freedom to maximum advantage in a race, but for now just be aware of this: The greatest advantage offered by a wetsuit is the freedom to slow down your arms, lengthen your body on each stroke, and end the frantic churning. If you happen to do some wetsuit swimming in pool or lake, focus more on slowing your arms and lengthening your body than on anything else, and recognize that you are imprinting the balanced-swimming form. Then when you swim without your wetsuit, try to keep the same feeling of leisure, control, and flow.

* * *

Just as a balanced body fights the water less, the laws of physics also say that a longer body will slip through the water more easily than a shorter one. And, happily, there are ways to make our bodies "longer" too — at least as far as the water is concerned. So now that you've mastered balance, it's time to start "Swimming Taller."

Chapter 6

How to Swim Taller: Regardless of Your Height

As with balance, "swimming taller" is neither natural nor instinctive; in coaching thousands of triathletes, I've seen only a few who swam taller without having been taught. But, as with the other Fishlike skills, knowing how to lengthen your "vessel" in the water can be learned by anyone, given the right kind of practice.

The most significant advantage to swimming taller is that the extra length makes your body more *slippery*. According to Froude's Law, as you increase the length of a vessel at the waterline, wave drag decreases and energy cost goes down. And though it may be a stretch to compare a 60-foot steel hull making 20 knots in open seas to a six-foot triathlete trying to make one meter/second in Kona Cove (and whose "vessel" is continually shape-morphing with each stroke), there is no doubt swimmers can benefit greatly from trying to be more "Froude worthy."

The payoff is clear. If you watched the finals of the 100-meter freestyle at the 2000 Olympics, you might have noticed something striking about the finalists: They look like they would make a pretty decent basketball team. In fact, the fastest men averaged about 6'5" while the fastest women were 5'10" or taller.

Common sense suggests several advantages of being taller: Longer arms to win close touch-outs. Long legs to turn a bit farther from the wall. Incremental advantages like those would help in a close race, but the more critical reason is that the maximum speed of a human swimmer is approximately one body length per second. All things being equal, this gives a 6'6" swimmer an advantage of approximately 10 yards over a 6'0" swimmer in a one-minute race. Thus, the price of admission to a final where everyone swims about two meters per second (48 to 49 seconds for 100 meters) is a body that's about two meters tall. And where do 6-footers find success? Generally, in events where the winning time might be only 1.7 to 1.8 meters per second, such as the 400- or 1500-meter freestyle.

Most triathletes are not endowed with unusual height, nor can they expect another growth spurt, but luckily this is not really a handicap in triathlon – as it would be if you harbored a secret goal to swim the 100-meter final in the next Olympics. The point is to do all you can to maximize the speed potential of the body you *do* have and to take back the advantage from taller rivals who haven't learned how to use their height to full advantage.

Here's why this works: Drag increases exponentially as we go faster; thus it takes a HUGE increase in power to swim faster if nothing else changes. But it is in your power to change the equation: Keeping your bodyline *as long as possible for as long as possible* during each stroke cycle is among the simplest things you can do to reduce drag. And anything you do to reduce drag hugely reduces the power required to swim at any speed. The less power and energy it takes you to swim, say, 28 minutes for 1500 meters, the better you'll feel on the bike and run.

Here's how you do it in freestyle:

1. Hide your head and swim "downhill." First things first. Keep working on your primary balance cues until you feel a clear sense of a "weightless arm" before you actually start *trying* to swim taller. Remember, if you haven't mastered balance and learned to make the water support you, your arms will be so busy trying to keep you afloat that you won't be able to use them to lengthen your body.

2. Lengthen your body with each stroke. As you swim, instead of thinking "Stroke...Stroke...Stroke," think "Reach...Reach...*Reach*." You'll still be stroking — the right arm strokes as the left arm reaches, and vice versa — but your focus will shift to the reaching arm, which has far more potential to increase speed and reduce drag. This will change the entire focus of your swimming, away from pushing water toward your feet (concentrating on what's happening *under* your body) to lengthening your body (concentrating on what's happening *in front* of your body). And that shift in focus will reduce your level of perceived effort. If you imagine you're sliding your arm through the sleeve of a jacket, you'll have it about right.

Use your arms to lengthen your vessel.

3. Reach *through*, not *over*, the water. Slice your hand into the water fairly close to your head, then extend it just below the surface. Reaching over the water is more natural, but a hand in the air is a weighted object that makes balance more difficult. Moreover, it does nothing to increase the length of your vessel at the waterline (remember Froude). But extending your hand just below the surface gives you that extra length. To get this right, practice this while doing your TI freestyle "overswitch" drills, and later while swimming:

- Have your hand *barely* clear the water on recovery.
- Slide your hand back into the water almost directly in front of your nose.
- Re-enter the water as if trying to cut a hole in the water with your fingertips and slip the rest of your arm *cleanly* through that hole.

4. Reach with a "weightless" arm. If all your brain cells are shouting "Reach!" as your hand enters the water, but your hand still plunges toward the bottom as it enters, there are two possible reasons: either you haven't solved your balance problem (in which case, see #1 or review Chapter 5), or the force of habit is still too powerful. If it's the latter, you can correct it by a little creative self-deception: Pretend each stroke is your last of the lap, and reach forward as if for the wall before you begin the stroke. This will help you form a new habit of extending your hand weightlessly, effortlessly, and unhurriedly before stroking, as if it was just floating out in front of you.

Slice your hand in close to your head.

5.   Use shoulder roll to extend your hand. Though you may feel as if your arm is weightless, don't feel as if it's disembodied. Use your arm as an extension of your torso. Work on this by extending each arm until you feel that shoulder touch your jaw; men with a bit of chin stubble should finish each practice with a small red spot inside each shoulder. An added dividend: More body roll will add an inch or two to your reach — and to the length of your vessel.

6.   Learn the "Switch," and practice "FQS." Swimming taller means you should always have one hand in front of your head — particularly at slower speeds — which also means that for a brief moment in each stroke cycle *both* hands should be in front of your head. This is known as Front-Quadrant Swimming (FQS), though many people confuse it with catch-up swimming (a non-TI drill in which the recovering hand touches the extended hand before each stroke).

As the photos show, our object is to learn to time strokes precisely so that one hand remains extended for slightly longer in each stroke, until the other hand is just about to enter the water. The quickest and easiest way to learn this is with our series of "Switch" drills, found on the video *Freestyle and Backstroke: The Total Immersion Way* and in Chapter 10.

7. Master one skill at a time. Swimming taller in freestyle involves more coordination than in other strokes. Avoid mental overload by learning the six stroke modifications just one at a time, in the order listed. Mastery of one will lead naturally to the next. Spend 10 to 20 minutes of each practice on one skill, and focus on only one or two skills in each session. Allow yourself at least two to three weeks to incorporate each skill. Most important, don't rush to practice them in whole-stroke swimming. Start with drills, then a mix of drill and swim. When you do begin whole-stroke practice, focus on only one point a time. *Whenever* you swim, never push off a wall without knowing what skill you are really trying to do well.

A Note on Front-Quadrant Swimming

Among the many non-traditional recommendations in the first Total Immersion book, the most-debated was for Front-Quadrant Swimming — mainly with regard to sprint swimming. Some critics have pointed out that, at top speed, sprinters usually don't race with both hands in front of their head (though most of the fastest middle-distance and distance swimmers do). And it's true that swimmers who practice FQS too rigidly can find themselves restricted from reaching the stroke rates necessary to swim fast in 50- and 100-meter races. So let's clarify how you can find out if it's really advantageous for your swimming and, if so, how to apply it properly.

Because this book is written for triathletes, it's important to point out that freestyle sprinters race at a stroke rate (SR) of up to 100 armstrokes per minute, while the best SR for most triathletes is just 50 to 60 strokes (25 to 30 stroke cycles) per minute. At that SR, it should be quite easy to maintain FQS (or semi-catch-up) timing with no sense of restricting your ability to swim freely and rhythmically. But even so, we always encourage swimmers to experiment with a range of stroke timing at a variety of speeds and stroke counts to find the timing that feels best to you. Here's how to do that.

Finding Your Best Stroke Timing

At TI workshops, we describe FQS as the most "negotiable" of the skills we teach. Practicing the Switch drills that teach FQS timing will allow you to discover for yourself whether you can make FQS feel comfortable and natural. A small percentage (less than 10%) of all the students I've worked with have found that FQS timing inhibited their natural sense of rhythm. We advised them to use the Switch drills to add just a bit more *awareness* of length to their strokes without disrupting their natural rhythms in whole-stroke swimming.

For the great majority — and particularly the slower-stroking triathletes — who can adopt FQS with a rhythm that feels comfortable, I explain that this is nonetheless still a *practice* strategy for imprinting timing that is not natural or instinctive. Do a good job of that by purposefully and consciously working on FQS at lower speeds in training, and when you start chasing the pack on race day, the nervous system will just know how to maintain the greatest efficiency at what feels like an appropriate and sustainable SR. You'll be able to swim freely at the stroke rates and rhythms that move you fastest.

What about those of you who might like to swim a short freestyle event in a Masters meet? Is it true that FQS doesn't work if you need to swim really fast? I can only say that I personally watched Alexander Popov for a cumulative total of several hours, both in meet warmup/warmdowns and in practice, while he was in New York for the 1998 Goodwill Games. Other coaches I know have also observed Popov's practices during his visits to the USA, for anywhere from a couple of hours to three weeks. And we all observed the same thing: He swam most of his practice laps relatively slowly with impeccable form, and every stroke on those slower laps was done with FQS timing.

The payoff comes on race day when, as a result of this rigorous nervous-system training in practice, Popov maintains greater stroke length at his highest stroke rate than do swimmers who fail to practice FQS. That's also why he held his form better in the closing stages of races, and won so many races over the final 10 to 15 meters.

I wanted the sprinters I coached at West Point to be able to do that too, so here's how we got the best out of FQS while ensuring they had the necessary SR for short races. At super-slow practice paces, we consciously practiced the greatest degree of overlap or FQS timing. As the pace increased, we gave up overlap bit by bit, trying to hold on to as much as possible without feeling restricted. I instructed them, as they approached race pace and race tempo, to just do what feels most natural.

The results, over the course of each six-month season during my three years coaching at West Point, were undeniable: a significant improvement in the SL my swimmers were able to maintain at their highest speeds. And by season's end they invariably swam *significantly* faster, and with significantly improved SL. As a long-distance open-water swimmer myself, I have used exactly the same approach in my own training

I can tell you from personal experience that it doesn't just work for the youngest and fastest among us, either. Over several years, I have been able to steadily reduce the number of strokes it takes me to swim 100 yards at super-slow speeds (from 52 to 39), to gradually improve my speed at every stroke count (13 spl, 14 spl, etc.), and have dropped my SPL in mile races in the pool from 19/20 to 15/16. This progressive increase in Stroke Length and economy has made me feel much more smooth and controlled at my top speeds. Best of all, it has helped minimize speed loss over my 12 years of Masters racing, from age 38 to 50.

You're almost fishlike. You've improved balance to save energy, letting the water do work that you once struggled to do. And you've reduced drag with a longer vessel so more of your energy goes into speed instead of making waves. All that's left is the final stage of the metamorphosis: learning how to slip through the smallest possible hole in the water.

Chapter 7

Slippery Swimming: The Smarter Way to Speed

I began swimming with aspiration upon entering my first race at age 15 in 1966. As soon as speed replaced fun as the goal of my pool time, I became aware of the gospel: "Swimming is hard." Virtually everything I've heard or read on swimming since has described the price of speed as "more" and "harder." No surprise then that the whole world understands the swimming speed problem in the same way.

Fortunately the whole world has it wrong. The one non-negotiable, unavoidable, unyielding limit to speed is *resistance*, not your capacity for long or hard work. There is no workout, wet or dry, that can overcome the amount of drag produced by your body as it travels through the water.

Consider this: Even Ian Thorpe or Alexander Popov, who swim as efficiently as a human can (gliding 25 yards in as few as six or seven freestyle strokes), use — at best — 10 percent of their energy for propulsion. More than 90 percent is consumed by wavemaking and other inefficiencies. What about athletes who take 22 or more strokes per 25-yard length? They may be spending as much as 97 percent of their energy making waves.

If you're one of the countless triathletes who find swimming exhausting or frustrating, it's a virtual certainty that drag, not your fitness, is to blame. It's drag that limits human-swimming speed to 5 mph or less, while some fish hit 50 mph with seeming ease. Fish are so much faster because evolution has shaped them to minimize drag. Arm-thrashing, leg-churning humans are almost as ideally designed to *maximize* drag. And no matter how conscientiously you streamline, just the fact that you swim "like a human" still creates a huge amount of water resistance. But a strategy like one that already works well for you in cycling can make a big difference.

I've enjoyed cycling for about 40 years, and have always had a general understanding that I could ride more easily when I was tucked over the handlebars than when I was "tall in the saddle." But I didn't fully appreciate how powerfully drag could influence cycling speed until I read that relatively little of a cyclist's energy output actually makes the wheels turn; most of it is spent pushing air out of the way. Thus, as every triathlete knows, a great deal of cycling speed can be created simply by lessening air resistance, instead of laboring to build leg power or aerobic conditioning.

I recall precisely when I realized drag must be an even bigger factor in swimming. In 1978 in Midlothian, Virginia, I began coaching at a pool with an underwater window. The first time I climbed down to watch my team during a set, I was spellbound by a graphic picture that had eluded me all the years I'd watched swimming from above. Watching my swimmers push off the wall, I could see that the tightly streamlined ones traveled a *looooong* way before they began stroking. They really looked like fish in an aquarium — so long as they were in streamline. The moment they began pulling and kicking, they worked much harder and moved much slower.

Those who maintained a sleek shape could cover up to eight fast and easy yards before they took their first stroke. Any swimmer not tightly molded into a torpedo shape lost speed so dramatically that they looked exactly as if they'd run into a wall. And they had. To a poorly streamlined body, the water is a wall. I understood, in that instant, that the primary thing limiting how fast my swimmers could go was not the workouts I spent hours devising, but the effect of drag on their bodies. Clearly the most valuable skill to teach was streamlining — not just on the pushoff, but the whole length of the pool.

This was a logical conclusion, based on the fact that water is over 800 times denser than the "thin" air that costs cyclists such a stunning amount of energy. In a medium as thick as water, the payoff for reducing drag at even the slowest speeds can be enormous. And water gets "thicker" as you go faster: Drag increases exponentially as speed goes up, so the payoff for *avoiding* drag also increases exponentially the better you avoid it.

Why Water Is a Wall

Boats, cars, and planes avoid drag best when they are long, sleek, and tapered. Humans can enjoy a moment or two of that as we push off, but as soon as we begin stroking again, most of us revert to blocky and angular shapes. (Seeing these shapes for the first time on slow-motion underwater video is an incredibly revealing moment for students at TI workshops.) Fast swimmers maintain the most streamlined position as they stroke; slow swimmers do not. *This is the most important distinction between them.*

But drag isn't just some general retarding force. There are three distinct forms of drag, which you can avoid better by understanding them. Two can be minimized by changes in technique, one by changing your suit.

1. Form drag is resistance caused by your human-body shape. As you swim, you push water in front of you, creating an area of higher pressure. Behind you, your body leaves a turbulent swirl, creating an area of lower pressure. Higher pressure in front and lower pressure behind creates a vacuum that, in effect, sucks you back. (That's why drafting off other swimmers — or cyclists — feels so much easier. The low-pressure area trailing the swimmer in front of you sucks you forward.) Form drag increases as the square of your velocity. Thus, twice as fast means four times as much form drag.

Your body's size and shape determine form drag, and the best way to minimize that drag is to *pierce* the water or slip through the smallest possible "hole." You do that by staying in a balanced, horizontal position and by making sure any side-to-side movement is rotation — not snaking or fishtailing. TI Coach Emmett Hines puts it succinctly: "If you're perfectly streamlined — as in the pushoff — *any* motion will increase form drag." That means it's critical, once you begin swimming after the pushoff, to make your propelling actions as smooth and economical as possible. Concentrate, even as you pull and kick, on fitting through the smallest possible hole in the water, and you'll be on the right track.

And, while swimming freestyle, you're at your sleekest when you spend most of each stroke cycle on your side, particularly in the brief interval between strokes. But doing that requires an impeccable sense of dynamic balance and side balance.

2. Wave drag. Just like a boat, you leave a wake while swimming. Wave drag is the resistance caused by the waves or turbulence you create. As Hines quips, "Making waves takes energy — all of it supplied by you. "The bigger your wake, the greater your energy loss. Unlike form drag, which increases as the square of velocity, wave drag increases as its cube. So as you double your speed, energy spent on wavemaking increases eightfold.

A long stroke and sleek bodyline create less wake and less drag.

A rushed stroke with too much kick creates more wake and more drag.

The key factor in wave drag is how smoothly you stroke. A rough, choppy, or rushed stroke increases turbulence, and turbulent water increases resistance. That's one of the reasons a long stroke is such an advantage: It lets you use a slower, more controlled turnover at any speed, which in turn means less turbulence, fewer waves — and less drag.

3. **Surface drag** is friction between the water and your skin. No technique can change this law of nature, but you can affect how it applies to you by wearing the right suit. Shed your billowy boxers for a skin-tight suit, and just feel the huge difference it makes. Racers, as you probably know, also shave down, and on top of that may don special racing suits of Teflon-like fabrics to reduce surface drag further still. So slippery is the material when compared to skin, that an increasing number of elite (and many sub-elite) competitors now wear styles that cover more and more of the body. For the rest of us, however, a well-fitting lycra suit will do the trick.

Tuning in to Drag

Besides the drag-defeating strategies noted above, the simplest and best strategy for slipping more easily through that wall of water is to pay attention to it. Alexander Popov may be the world's fastest swimmer, but he often practices swimming "super slowly" at speeds where he can feel the resistance trying to hold him back, so he can figure out how to minimize it. Even without Popov's super-sensitive "drag antennae" to pick up signals, there are ways you can heighten your own sensitivity to it:

First, intentionally create more drag. Push off the wall with your arms wide and head high. Feel the resistance. Then push off in the most streamlined position, and notice how much it's reduced. Use that "awareness training" in your regular swimming to recognize the ways in which the water resists you, and to the stroke changes — such as keeping your head in a neutral position — that enable you to feel less of it.

Second, use your ears. Tune in to how much noise you make while swimming. Do you splash, plop, or plunk? Sound is energy, and the less of your mechanical energy you convert into noise, the more remains to move you forward. More to the point, anything that results in noisy swimming is evidence of inefficiency. Working on "silent swimming" is one of the best ways to tune in more acutely to how you're flowing through the water, and can help you improve your fluency.

Third, use your eyes. Are there bubbles in your stroke? Goggles make it easy to tell, and marathon swimmer and TI coach Don Walsh uses his to observe one of the most available pieces of "swimming knowledge" you can have about yourself. In fact for a full year of practice, Don thought more about eliminating bubbles than about anything else and credits that focus with helping him complete the 28.5-mile Manhattan Island Marathon in *14,000* fewer strokes than his rivals.

Don Walsh gliding around Manhattan.

That number is no figment. Walsh actually calculated it, by having his boat crew monitor his stroke rate and compare it with that of other swimmers. He swam just as fast at 50 strokes per minute as other swimmers did at about 72. That means in the nine hours it took Walsh to swim up the East River and down the Hudson, he took something on the order of 27,000 strokes, while other swimmers in the race — including many who finished behind him — ended up needing about 41,000! That many strokes would have sent Don halfway around Manhattan again! Viewed another way, he got a "free ride" of almost 10 miles by being so slippery. If you could learn to slip through the water rather than battling it, you'll see far fewer bubbles, and there will be much less turbulence in your wake.

Finally, imagine your body has a kind of shadow trailing behind you as you swim. Remember: You're creating a wake similar to that of a boat, and though it spreads a bit as it reaches your feet, it doesn't spread much. Consider that wake your shadow, and anything that slips outside it as drag. Your feet, for instance, may be helping you along as you kick, but as soon as they slip outside your "shadow," they increase drag.

The Choice Is Yours

You have a choice to make each time you arrive at the pool: Spend your time training hard and long to muscle up your propulsive force and inflate your aerobic capacity, or focus on trimming drag and reducing the energy spent making waves. A trip to any aquarium will show you the smarter path is the path of least resistance.

Up to this point we've been focusing on good "vessel design," exploring all the ways to stay balanced, long, and sleek. Now that your "hull" is as efficient as it can be, it's time to tune up your engine to run with the same, smart efficiency.

"95-Mph Freestyle" — Effortless Power from the Core

So far, our strategy for mastering fast, fluent, "fishlike" swimming has focused on minimizing resistance — not on maximizing propulsion. But once you've conquered drag, you can create new efficiencies by learning to tap an effortless power source as you stroke. The good news is that the eliminating skills you learned to minimize drag are the same skills you'll use to maximize propulsion. You just think about them differently and apply them in different ways.

Over time, all the counterintuitive things you've learned you must do in a concentrated way to be Fishlike — hiding your head, pressing your "buoy," lengthening your vessel — will gradually grow into habits. As they do, you'll be able to shift some of your brainpower to making your propelling actions smooth, controlled, and fluent. The first step is to learn to use your most effortless power source: the core body.

You'll see the most persuasive argument for that by visiting an aquarium. Watching fish under water makes it clear that the best "engine" for propulsion in a fluid is the core body. Lacking arms and legs, fish can't propel by pulling and kicking; they use rhythmic body undulation or oscillation to move with stunning speed, grace, and ease. Watch from poolside (or on TV) at an elite-level meet and you'll see the world's best swimmers apply the same principle: The torso sets the rhythm and the arms and legs synchronize with it. Then watch lap swimmers at your pool. Most do just the opposite: arms flail, legs churn, and the core body isn't involved or works at cross-purposes.

So, let's begin a whole-body tune-up of your power train, from the engine (your torso) to the propellers (your hands).

The Kinetic Chain: Power from the Core

It's only natural to think of our arms and legs as the "engine" for fast swimming. When we want to go faster, we instinctively work them harder and faster. And when swimmers devote countless yards to pulling with a foam buoy immobilizing their legs, or kicking with arms holding a board, they're reinforcing these instincts in their muscle memory. The shift from arm-dominated to core-based propulsion will take time, patience, persistence, and attention. But I promise the rewards will be more than worth it.

If you *really* want to learn to swim like a fish, consider again how fish actually swim. They scoot through the water in a most uncomplicated way, by rhythmically oscillating or undulating the entire body, which produces tail-whip, and off they go. Fishlike propulsion for humans is based on the same principle: core-body rotation for long-axis strokes (freestyle and backstroke), undulation for the short-axis strokes of butterfly and breaststroke.

In an ideal world it wouldn't be necessary for swimmers to *learn* hip rotation. Rolling from side to side is already the most natural way for your body to accommodate the alternating-arm action of freestyle. Prove it to yourself by standing in place and moving your arms as if swimming freestyle. Roll your hips and you move freely; keep them immobile and you feel restricted. Because rolling is a natural accommodation, a freestyler must actually expend energy to remain flat (usually by splaying the arms or legs). This isn't usually intentional; swimmers remain flat because they haven't mastered side-lying balance. As soon as they become comfortable with side-lying balance — something not natural or instinctive in most people but which can be learned — they stop fighting themselves and roll more freely.

Though coaches speak of hip rotation as a way to swim more powerfully, in truth it has an even greater advantage: As I explained in the last chapter, your body slips through the water more easily in the side-lying position. *Remember: Techniques that reduce drag are always more beneficial than those that increase power.*

But as you become more slippery by learning the balance that frees your body to roll, you also gain access to an incredibly powerful "engine" for swimming propulsion: the kinetic chain, the same power source that uncorks 95-mph fastballs. A baseball pitcher's power originates in the legs and gradually gets magnified as it travels up the chain for delivery to his pitching arm to uncork a blistering fastball.

The world's best swimmers know this instinctively. While inefficient swimmers use arms and shoulders to do most of the work, Olympic swimmers get their power in the torso and use their arms and shoulders mainly to transmit this force to the water. Great technique can be a great equalizer: Mastery of the kinetic chain is what allows Tiger Woods, for example, to drive a golf ball farther than rivals who are bigger and stronger. It also provides the power for nearly any kind of hitting or throwing motion.

The kinetic chain is not a complicated concept. In fact, you probably learned naturally to use it, many years ago, on a playground swing. I hazily recall starting with vigorous leg kicking, which just made the swing shake a bit, but certainly not soar. But I can vividly recall how satisfying it was when I began to figure it out and experienced, for the first time, the effect of engaging *every* muscle in finely timed, coordinated action. If I leaned forward slightly, the swing would move back a little. As gravity pulled it down again, I helped it along by leaning back. Each time gravity reversed me, I added enough leverage to make it go a little farther. And farther, and farther.

The most thrilling moment was when I reached the apogee of the backward swing, having figured out how to put *all* my muscle and mass into a perfectly linked series of arcs. The simple desire to go higher and faster taught me to pull on the chain with my hands and tighten my stomach muscles to link the tension of my backward-pulling arms to the stretching toes of my forward-straining legs, adding my power to the accelerating force of gravity. This skill, simple enough to be learned by any child, produced a breathtakingly powerful swoop through space, with such marvelous efficiency that I could continue endlessly without tiring. Engaging the kinetic chain, when you get it right, can be an addictive experience. It's no less so for your swimming, when you learn to use it fully. Effortless power for fishlike swimming is produced in much the same way. Energy for the most powerful movements ripples through our bodies like a cracked whip until it finally arrives at its release point. In freestyle and backstroke, body rotation provides a big chunk of the power — as it does when we throw a rock, a javelin, or a karate blow. In all these cases, the legs and hips power the torso, which in turn drives the arm. In the body undulation of butterfly and breaststroke, the arms are powered simultaneously by a "force coupler" in which core muscles link hips and shoulders in the same way as when you're doing a pullup, double-poling on skis...or soaring on a playground swing.

And linking your effort to the force of gravity, as you do on a playground swing, also works extremely well when swimming freestyle. The rhythmic body rolling, which sends power to your stroke, is aided by the same kind of gravity-assisted weight shifts you use in cross-country skiing and in-line skating. These weight shifts, triggered by the timing of Front-Quadrant Swimming, are fairly easy to learn by diligently practicing the "Switch" drills in the TI learning sequence. Here are the steps you can follow to link the engine of the Kinetic Chain to your stroke:

1. **Learn side lying balance.** Until you are completely comfortable being on your side and rolling freely from one side to the other, you'll probably swim too flat, which disables the kinetic chain. Practice Drill 2 in Lesson One and Drill 3 in Lesson Two to become completely comfortable on your side.

2. **Improve your dynamic balance.** Stay slippery by maintaining a needle shape. Breathe by rolling that needle shape to where the air is. Propel by rolling that needle shape rhythmically back and forth. You begin to set this dynamic process in motion by practicing Drill 4 in Lesson Two and Drill 5 in Lesson Three.

3. **Learn to use gravity to trigger the kinetic chain.** The timing of Front-Quadrant Swimming will teach you how to use gravity and stroke timing to your advantage. You learn this by practicing the "switch" drills in Lessons Four and Five.

Learn FQS timing with switch drills.

4. Keep the core body central to your swimming with purposeful whole-stroke practice. Once you've learned the basic skills with drills as suggested, it's still important to reinforce the principles of the drills in your whole-stroke sets. You need to fight the instincts that can take you back to too much reliance on arms and legs. Some helpful focal points that can be helpful include:

- Swim with your whole body. Any time you feel your stroke breaking down into an unconnected mess, or just becoming a bit sloppy, concentrate on the feeling of swimming with your whole body, with your arms connected to the action of the torso.
- Put your weight on your armpit. As you enter and extend each hand — as if down a sleeve — through the water, complete your extension by leaning into your armpit. This will help ensure that you finish the weight shift.
- Think about your third eye. You can also accentuate your body rotation by thinking of your belly button as a third eye and imagine looking at each side wall with it on every stroke cycle.

5.   Accentuate your use of the kinetic chain with LA Combo.
"Purposeful exaggeration" can help imprint any skill more deeply. You
can exaggerate body roll by rolling 360 degrees from time to time while
swimming. Doing Long-Axis Combinations, alternating cycles of freestyle
and backstroke, either drilling or swimming, is guaranteed to make any
swimmer roll more. See the video *Freestyle and Backstroke: The Total
Immersion Way* for more information on how to do this.

One of the things most likely to interfere with your use of the kinetic chain for propulsion is overeager use of your arms to muscle through
the water. Since we've already provided another power source for propulsion, freeing the arms and shoulders of that job, let's see how you can use
your arms simply to deliver the power your body provides.

Chapter 9

A New Role for Your Hands: Standing Still

Most swimmers believe that stroke technique means "how you push water back with your hands," and give that motion most of their attention. Working on "technique" therefore means tweaking the armstroke, and "power" means putting more force and acceleration into it. Between what instinct suggests, and traditional instruction reinforces, the hands do seem to be 90% of swimming.

Most swimming books also share a keen fascination with hand movements, reporting in staggering detail on angle of attack, sweeps, pitches, vectors, lift forces, etc. The hands of gifted swimmers unquestionably *do* move in highly nuanced ways. But while that information may have academic interest, its practical value is nil. The movements described happen so quickly that no swimmer can consciously control the adjustments needed to get them just right. And elite swimmers don't get their wonderful technique from reading those books; they just do what *feels* best. You can acquire a lot of that advantageous *feel* by following the advice in this chapter.

But understand this: Even if swimmers did have the concentration and precise muscular control to make the fine adjustments to get the hand pattern just right, at the end of the day it's still just a little hand pushing against *water*...trying to propel a big body through a resistant medium. Always minimize drag first.

Learn to "Anchor" Your Hands

My mentor, Coach Bill Boomer, once said: "Your hips are the engine for swimming; your hands are just the propellers." And one of the surest ways to disconnect your propeller from its engine is overly aggressive stroking. A "controlled" stroke, one that stays connected to its power source through its full length, is one that begins with an "anchored" hand.

On land, the power-producing kinetic chain starts from a fixed (or "anchored") point — feet planted on the ground. You begin by twisting the body away from the intended direction of the movement — e.g., rearing back to throw a baseball or taking a backswing in golf. With the feet fixed in place, you get an effect known as elastic loading, similar to stretching a rubber band. The cocked hip then acts like a whip handle, throwing energy upward through torso, shoulders, and arms, with increasing speed and power.

With no foot-to-ground anchor, a swimmer's hips cannot act as a whip handle. But they can deliver power by working as a unit with the torso and arms. Still, the process must start with an anchoring point to create that fingers-to-toes band of engaged muscle we used to such dynamic effect on the playground swing. In fishlike swimming that power-linkage starts with an "anchored hand." While your instincts tell you to grab water and push it back *hard*, you can actually tap far more effortless power by extending your hand fully, and then just *holding on to your place* in the water — as if grasping a rung on a ladder — rather than hurriedly pushing back. Try to make your hand stand still, then let the kinetic chain roll you past the spot where your hand is anchored.

This was first observed in 1970, when famed Indiana University coach Doc Counsilman filmed swimming legend Mark Spitz, the world's greatest swimmer at the time, with an underwater camera. Attaching tiny lights to Spitz's hands to highlight their movements, Counsilman shot him from the side, against a gridlike backdrop. When he viewed the film at slow motion, Counsilman was startled to see that Spitz's hands exited the water *forward* of where they had entered. Spitz could not possibly be pushing his hands back, if they came out ahead of their entry point.

Nor could Jackie Hatherly, a 35-year-old Ironman qualifier from Toronto, who attended a TI workshop in April, 2000 and who quickly developed one of the most fishlike strokes we've ever seen. Watching from the side on underwater video on the second day, it was obvious that her hands entered and exited at the same place, while her body slid sleekly past their anchoring point on each stroke. Small wonder that she swam 25 meters freestyle in 11 strokes, after taking 17 strokes to swim the same distance just a day earlier.

Learn to "Feel the Water"

Training yourself to make your hand stand still rather than pushing it back does seem odd. How can your body go in one direction unless your hand goes the other? Admittedly, the water doesn't offer a convenient grip. But when you develop an acute "feel of the water," you can use your grip on the water to move yourself forward very nearly as a rock climber uses his hold on the rock to move upward. Coaches often describe "feel of the water" as a prize with a staggering price. They can't define it *exactly*, but suggest you must have been born with a gift for controlling elusive water molecules...or must spend millions of yards patiently acquiring this special knack.

There is no doubt that most elite swimmers have a variety of gifts that help them perform on a higher plane, and "feel of the water" is among the most important. But it's not difficult to explain. It's simply a heightened ability to sense minute differences in water pressure, and maximize that pressure with the body's propelling surfaces while minimizing it with the rest of the body. There is also no doubt that feel of the water *can* be an acquired skill. And it needn't take years to acquire. Here's how you can get a better grip on the ability to hold the water:

1.   **Get the catch right.** Swimmers usually give about 90 percent of their technique focus to the armstroke, and by now you know I think that's a poor use of your brainpower, preferring you pay more attention to drag because that brings faster, better results. But, when you do focus on propelling actions (mainly after you are balanced, tall, slippery, and moving fluently), give 90% of that attention to the "catch." Focus on your hands while they're in front of your head (see below for guidance), and once they've

passed your shoulders, just let them fall off your mental radar screen. Once properly initiated, a stroke doesn't benefit from further guidance.

2.   Start each stroke by making your hands stand still. Your instincts tell you to grab the water and push back. Ignore them. Instead, teach yourself to make your hand stay in front while you bring your body over it. Yes, this is a difficult goal, but work at it patiently and mindfully anyway. Such efforts will help you resist the urge to muscle the water back.

3.   Drill, drill, drill. Learning a skill as elusive and refined as this takes a lot of concentration, the kind you get in drills, where you repeat simple movements with full attention instead of trying to tweak something that happens in a millisecond in whole-stroke swimming. The "Switch" drills in Lessons Three, Four, and Five teach you to connect your hands to your core body, and move them in perfect coordination. They also help you learn to anchor your hands and bring your body over them. To multiply the effect of any drills — but particularly drills used to teach anchoring — do them with the fistglove® stroke trainer (see pages 60 to 63).

4.   Swim super slowly. Drills teach you how things will feel when they're "right." When you begin to apply what you've learned in drills, you'll retain far more of that feeling if you swim verrry slowly. The more slowly you swim, the more "concentration space" you give yourself to cultivate a finer sense of water pressure on the catch. Just be patient. Leave your hand out in front of you. S-t-r-e-t-c-h that moment, pressing gently on the water until you feel the water return some of that pressure to your hands (another awareness hugely heightened by fistgloves®). And while you're swimming slowly...

5.   Count your strokes. A reduced stroke count is a simple, reliable indicator that you're *not* pulling back. If you've whittled your count for a single 25-yard pool length down to, say, 13 or fewer strokes, one of the things you're likely to be doing well is holding on to the water. As you go faster (and your stroke count increases) stay hyper-alert to any sense of water slippage, like a car spinning its wheels.

6.   Try to have slow hands. Compare the speed at which you sense your hands moving back, with how fast you feel your body moving forward. Try to have "slow hands and a faster body" or, at the very least, match the speed of your hands to the speed of your body. This is a great corrective any time you feel your stroke getting rough and ragged.

7. Last but not least... Teaching and my own training experience have convinced me that the most beneficial tool for acquiring *feel* is the fistglove® stroke trainer. I'll let Scott Lemley, their inventor, tell you about them.

The Fistglove® stroke trainer
How Those Little Black Gloves Can Lead to Huge Improvements in Your Stroke
By Scott Lemley

Scott Lemley has been coaching and teaching swimming for 20-plus years. He is currently head coach of the Midnight Sun Swim Team in Fairbanks, Alaska. As a longtime student and instructor in the martial art of Aikido, Scott observed that the key steps to mastering any martial art — finding your balance, focusing your mind, and relaxing your body — are the key steps to mastering any swimming stroke.

One aspect of martial-arts teaching that particularly intrigued Scott was the practice of blindfolding students to compel them to become receptive to sensory information derived from sources other than the eyes, to develop a whole-body sense of balance. Reasoning that "feel" with the hands was the swimming equivalent of the perspective gained through sight on land, Scott set about developing "a blindfold for the hands." The result was the fistglove® stroke trainer. Below, Scott explains some of the many benefits of training with fistgloves®.

Before becoming a swim coach I taught Aikido, a martial art that emphasizes relaxation. Aikido training taught me that the more I relaxed, the more self-aware I became and the more efficiently and quickly I could move. I adopted these same principles to my swim coaching and have made it a core goal to teach my swimmers to combine the ability to focus mentally while relaxing physically. I used fist swimming a fair amount, but also felt that I could improve that practice by finding a way to swim effortlessly with fists closed for longer periods without having to expend either mental or physical energy. I tested this theory on myself by duct-taping my hands closed and warming up that way for 30 minutes before swimming with "normal" hands.

As an unexpected benefit, for the first time I became acutely aware of my lack of balance, the pressure of the water on my forearms, and the "sharp edges" I exposed to the water's resistance as I pushed off. I also discovered that my hands became very sensitive to pressure **after** I removed the duct tape, allowing me to "hold on to the water" with far more nuanced technique. After I began taping my swimmers' hands, I observed that every swimmer gained noticeable fluidity in their strokes. Instead of having one or two "gifted" swimmers and a host of dedicated but "less gifted" swimmers, I soon had what I came to think of as a team full of dedicated **and** gifted swimmers. After experimenting with "taped" fists for 17 years, I finally designed, patented, and began to manufacture a prototype latex glove, which I named the "fistglove® stroke trainer."

Fistgloves® make you more aware of how balanced and streamlined you are.

Fistgloves®: How They Work

One essential in the acquisition of improved swim technique is our ability to change the way we interact with our environment. Humans seem to be "hardwired" to interact with the water in a particular way, but I believe we can change that in very significant ways. This is a constant theme underlying how I ask my swimmers to train. Using fistgloves® has given them unprecedented choice and control over how they interact with the water

I want my swimmers to be able to choose finesse over brute strength. When they make this choice, they swim best or near-best times with far greater consistency. But finesse in the water must be *taught*; it rarely comes naturally. Finesse has much to do with how we feel "pressure" on our hands. Reading this pressure is both a source of information and a distraction. Because we're instinctively "hand-dominant" when swimming, most of us are so fixated on what's happening with our hands that we tune out other body parts. As long as our hands feel the pressure of the water's resistive force, we figure we're "good to go" and proceed to push it toward our feet in a way that satisfies our palms and psyches — but often neglects our body position. Is our entire body balanced and streamlined to avoid drag? It's hard to tell if we are thinking only about our palms. Add to the hand-dominant theme our human proclivity to solve problems with force, and it's no wonder that we see a lot of manhandling the water.

Another pitfall of being a swimmer who gets satisfaction from feeling pressure against the hands (and the more the better), is that it's all too easy to think that being unbalanced and unstreamlined is OK — perhaps even *good*. After all, an unstreamlined body will encounter massive resistance, and that resistance will feel correct and productive to most swimmers. Pushing against a substance as dense as water gives us a great sense of accomplishment. All too often the only accomplishment is to burn calories. To truly swim well, we must learn how to "feel" the water with our entire body, not just the hands, and learn to find our balance and cease our endless struggling to plow ahead.

All humans have proprioceptors (specialized nerve endings) in our joints, muscles, and skin that give us constantly updated information on how our joints are angled, how fast we're moving our limbs, how our arms and legs are positioned relative to each other, and the pressure of the water against various body parts. This wealth of feedback can overwhelm us if we don't know how to process it — or can help us achieve balance and flow if we learn to organize it and use it correctly. Usually our brain is so busy processing the information coming from our eyes and hands that we're not conscious of being out of alignment or off balance in the water.

Wearing fistgloves® helps you make balance a priority. Attempting to swim for the first time without the use of your hands, you'll probably thrash around for 5 or 10 minutes, completely helpless. But your brain will seek to solve this new puzzle by using other sources of information and other means of locomotion. Almost automatically, you'll start to swim with more finesse and less brute force. With the fistgloves®, you *must* learn to be balanced and streamlined; otherwise, you'll make no forward progress in the pool.

After wearing the gloves for 30 minutes or so, swim with open hands. You'll immediately experience what we call the fistglove® effect — a rush of information from your previously constrained, but now highly sensitive, hands to your brain. The result is that you'll become very discriminating in terms of how you angle your hands against the water, instinctively choosing the angles that give maximum purchase on what is a pretty slippery medium. You'll also become ultra-sensitive to the importance of "gripping" the water instead of "slipping" through it.

The first 30 minutes spent wearing fistgloves® will make you more aware of how balanced and streamlined you are. The next 30 minutes swimming *without* the gloves will help you learn to "hold" the water better. Fistgloves® help us become more effective on both sides of the equation. Give them a try. I think you'll enjoy the experience.

Hi Terry,

I'm writing to tell you that the lessons of the workshop all came together a couple days ago and it was so exciting to feel it happening! John and I have been faithfully practicing four times a week, mainly balance drills, with some switch drills mixed in. Last week, we started to incorporate some swimming. I didn't feel the ease at first, but I focused on hiding my head and swimming downhill. On Sunday it clicked and I kept going and going and going! It was beautiful, effortless, and fun!

Before the workshop I could do only three pool lengths before I had to stop. Sunday, as soon as I could feel the balance, I did 40 lengths without stopping and felt great afterward. After a few laps, John stopped swimming and sat on the wall to watch me because he could tell something had changed. We've also noticed that other people actually stop their swimming to watch us practice; they seem intrigued by how quietly and smoothly we drill. Everyone else is splashing all around us and we are just flowing down the pool!

I was convinced the TI approach was right after reading the book but I was a little scared coming to the workshop since I was such a weak swimmer. However, I knew I had to learn the right way. I learned so much that weekend and received so much support and encouragement from the coaches. I never thought I would enjoy swimming so much; what I felt on Sunday was an experience of a lifetime. And I realize it is just the beginning. I'm going again tonight and can't wait to get into the pool!

We will think of you all when we get out of the water during our triathlons refreshed, not tired. Thank you again for your caring and knowledge; we are both so much better for it.
Sincerely,
Dottie (and John) O'Connor

The lesson: Stop just swimming and start LEARNING. And once you begin working on the drills, be patient in your practice. They WILL work if you give them time. And once they do, your new skills will take you far beyond where you might have gotten by just continuing to swim laps.

Part 3

The School for Fishlike Swimming

Up to this point, our focus has been conceptual: building a knowledge foundation that allows you to understand what constitutes good swimming and how you can swim better just by changing the shape of your "vessel." Now that you're "book-smart" about swimming, it's time to move our classroom to the pool and begin teaching your muscles. Over the course of six Total Immersion "swim lessons" and other guidance on how to teach yourself successfully, you will learn to swim in a completely new way that will be faster, easier, and more enjoyable. We will do this as if every person who picks up this book knows nothing at all about swimming. We've found that all of our students, no matter how much swimming they may already have done, progress much faster by starting with the most elementary skill and progressing logically through the whole sequence of TI drills. So let's get right to it.

BUT FIRST: The six lessons to follow contain exhaustively *detailed* instructions on how to do each drill in the TI freestyle learning sequence, and the text instructions are complemented by photos of the key positions. Still, as one of our students said, "If a picture is worth a thousand words, video must be worth 10,000 words." Short of being taught face-to-face by a TI Coach, the surest way to master 100% of the essential skills is to use the companion video, *Fishlike Freestyle: The Total Immersion Way*, as your primary guide to the fine points and desired movement quality. This video was produced as we put the finishing touches on this book and has been designed as the perfect complement to it. If you did not purchase the video in a package with the book, please refer to the Resources section in the back for order info.

Swimming As a Martial Art

Next time you visit the pool, spend 10 minutes watching other swimmers. What you'll see — even if you watch someone for 60 minutes — is that every stroke looks exactly the same. Which is just how you'd look to someone watching you. Your stroke is a habit pattern, deeply imprinted in your nervous system by thousands or millions of previous strokes. The phrase "practice makes perfect" gets it only partly right. "Practice makes permanent...whatever you happen to practice" is far truer.

As we switch from theory to practice, you're about to become your own coach and teacher. And your success will depend on practicing only the movements you'd like in your "muscle memory" and on scrupulously avoiding whatever you don't want imprinted there. "Tweaking" your present stroke, while trying to "stay in shape" with swim repeats, will limit your progress, because the imprint of millions of previous strokes is so resistant to change. Fortunately you now have a proven alternative.

Each year we teach about 2000 students in TI workshops. Their average stroke count at the beginning of the workshop is 21 to 22 for 25 yards. A day later that average has improved to 17 strokes for 25 yards, or an average gain in Stroke Length of 20 percent. This degree of improvement, following several hours of instruction, is stunning for people who may have swum 5 or 10 years with little noticeable change. The two primary reasons for such transcendent improvement are "muscle amnesia" and "martial-arts swimming." You can also create transformation by observing these two principles in your self-coaching.

Avoiding Struggle

After we videotape our students doing a length of freestyle on Saturday morning, they don't swim another length of whole-stroke freestyle until the final 10 to 15 minutes on Sunday afternoon — by which time they've spent about six hours practicing efficient swimming movements without a single "old" freestyle stroke. By then, most have replaced their old stroke with a new, improved stroke. By teaching with movements their nervous systems don't recognize as *swimming*, we've given them "muscle amnesia," a blank slate for learning new skills and bypassing old habits.

The second key to success is the "martial-arts swimming" part. Formal swimming instruction has existed for only 50 years or so, while martial arts have been taught and practiced for thousands of years, giving martial-arts masters considerably more opportunity to learn the best way to teach movement skills. Their non-negotiable rule is: "Avoid practicing movements you cannot perform correctly." Martial-arts students always start with positions and movements that seem ridiculously simple and progress through more challenging movements by small steps.

As they soon discover, movements that seem the simplest soon reveal great complexity and can be mastered on many levels. The more patiently they give themselves time to refine each step, the more fluent and effortless they become at higher-level skills. We'll guide you through the same kind of progression on the way to becoming a Fishlike swimmer.

Effective Tools for Self-Coaching

Here's one more thing to consider as you begin coaching yourself: Because of your human DNA, virtually everything you do instinctively in the water makes you less efficient; the skills that make you more economical won't come naturally. You'll need to make a mindful, organized, patient effort to make them as instinctive as the inefficient habits they'll replace.

Fortunately, TI Lessons offer a virtually foolproof process that is:

1. **Flexible.** Choose just the right degree of difficulty and continually adjust it to provide an appropriate challenge.

2. **Sequential.** Each step provides precisely the skill you'll need to tackle the next.

3. **Incremental.** Each step is just slightly more advanced than the previous one.

4. **Economical.** *Every* drill teaches you an ingredient essential to being fishlike in the whole stroke.

From the first lesson, you'll not only move through the water better but also enjoy it more. In fact, you should feel good *every* time you swim. And the ongoing challenge of maintaining fluency through progressively more complex movements will make swimming just as satisfying mentally as physically. This will help create and sustain what we call a *flow state*, an almost euphoric condition, similar to the "runner's high," in which you virtually lose yourself in the satisfaction of the activity.

Learning Vs. Training

Total Immersion has outperformed all other swim-improvement methods because each mini-skill becomes the springboard for a more advanced one in a smooth progression that gradually crystallizes into a well-formed stroke that doesn't need "spot fixing." The instinctive sense most swimmers have that whole-stroke swimming is the path to *better* whole-stroke swimming seldom allows them to achieve this nirvana because, for most people, whole-stroke swimming means "practicing struggle." Every length with poor form makes it that much harder to change to a smoother one. To learn a better way you have to actively unlearn the old way, by *never practicing it again*.

This process can actually help you reach your goal in a more direct way than elite swimmers — whose fluency and effortlessness look so unattainable — reached theirs. While these human fish have all had coaching, most have been guided mainly by their exceptional kinesthetic intuition. Over time, they've experienced countless breakthrough moments when their stroke felt just right, moments they immediately stored in muscle memory. Eventually, their skill library becomes comprehensive enough to produce an extremely smooth and highly efficient way of swimming.

But this process takes too long and — unless you're among the fortunate few with the right "gifts" — won't happen anyway. So TI takes this haphazard and prolonged process, and organizes it for you. With our step-by-step drill system, any swimmer can create flashes of insight, store them in muscle memory, and recapture them in a convenient and reliable way. And by practicing them repeatedly, the right movements become more natural, automatic, and integrated.

Eventually, when you resume whole-stroke swimming after polishing the basics in your drills, your nervous system has taken so many "snapshots" of sensations like those that elite swimmers instinctively feel, that it becomes easy for you to assemble them into a complete "movie." And because our natural efficiency in water is so limited to start with, there's virtually no "improvement ceiling" when it comes to good technique. Whether you're a beginner learning basics or swam competitively before taking up triathlon, if you practice TI, there will always be some new breakthrough in store. After 35 years of swimming and 29 of coaching, I still make exciting discoveries that make me feel better than ever in the water.

Taking a Break with Yoga Breathing

For years, I've seen coaches push their swimmers to do drills on challenging intervals. I've also seen swimmers on their own trying to do drills faster or with less rest. While grudgingly acknowledging that drills probably have value, they're still locked into "keeping up the yardage." So let me clarify once more: **The purpose of training is to maximize energy supply. The purpose of drilling is to minimize energy cost. Saving energy *always* produces greater improvement, faster, than training to increase it.** And, until you have elite-level skills, you *can't* focus on both fitness and fluency at the same time. Later, as I'll explain, you can integrate efficiency practice with forms of conditioning. But if you push to cover more distance in less time while drilling, you'll do neither well.

To reap all the benefits drills can provide, you must practice them in a calm, controlled environment. One proven way is to ignore the pace clock. When I'm most focused on efficiency, I never so much as glance at the clock. I'm utterly disinterested in how fast I may be going or what "training effect" I may be getting. I'm solely interested in how easily I slip through the water, how fluent and coordinated my movements feel, and how silently and splash-free I can move along.

But though I make no use of the pace clock, I still want some way to ensure that my students get enough rest to keep their heart rate in a moderate aerobic state that allows attentive, meticulous movement. We do that by using deep, relaxing "yoga breaths" for rest and recovery. They bring two restorative advantages: They normalize breathing, which helps keep your heart rate down. They also "center" you mentally and psychologically, reducing distraction and improving concentration.

Recover During Each Lap

The technique is simple: Inhale deeply, then let your breath fall out. Relax a moment before inhaling again. You can regulate your rest easily by increasing or decreasing the number of yoga breaths taken before your next exercise or repeat. While teaching, I recommend that students take at least three breaths while pausing in Sweet Spot, between cycles, as they are learning the drills. Later, they can decrease to one or two yoga breaths in Sweet Spot to make their drill rhythm more "swimming-like." Increasing the Sweet-Spot pause to as many as five or seven breaths will turn any drill into something of a kicking exercise. This will be a far more valuable way to practice kicking than, say, kicking with a Styrofoam board. But, if you take fewer breaths be careful not to reduce to the point where you feel rushed or confused.

Recover at the Wall

We also use yoga breaths to regulate the rest taken at the wall between repeats or pool lengths. When teaching, I also recommend at least three yoga breaths between each pool length, so long as you're in the learning phase for any new drill. Again, the amount of rest taken can be easily regulated by increasing or decreasing the number of breaths. Are you feeling slightly breathless or do you sense fatigue affecting the quality of your movements? Just add breaths. Or take fewer, if you can drill impeccably with less rest. On longer reps, say, 50s, rather than 25s, you might increase your rest interval from 3 breaths to perhaps 5. Once you've had a chance to experiment with the yoga-breathing interval, you'll find it the simplest way to adjust your rest period as finely as you want...while bringing the additional dividend of improved concentration to a style of swimming that *always* benefits from more acute attention.

Recover Anytime

Yoga breathing in Sweet Spot has proven effective as a way of reducing heart rate and restoring control in any number of circumstances. Many TI swimmers use it as a way of resting in the middle of an open-water or triathlon swim. They continue stroking and breathing rhythmically for as long as they feel in control and able to sustain their pace and effort. If, at any time, they feel themselves getting ragged or inefficient or simply want a moment to collect their wits, they just roll to Sweet Spot and breathe until they feel restored. This gives them, in effect, a "pool wall" in the middle of open water. Once they feel restored, they just roll to the nose-down (Skating) position and resume smooth, controlled stroking. (See more on this in Chapter 21.)

And finally, as you'll see, we use the Sweet Spot and yoga breaths as a means of easing the transition from drilling to continuous whole-stroke swimming with rhythmic breaths. If your seamless rhythmic breaths are going well, then just keep at it. If your form breaks down, take a break in Sweet Spot, then resume rhythmic breathing.

If you're like me, you'll soon find yourself using breaths as your recovery device in other activities. I first learned the technique when taking yoga classes and quickly realized its value for swimming. Now I use them in all manner of exercise — from governing how long I hold a stretching position (usually 10 to 30 breaths) to varying my yoga practice from more meditative (more breaths in each position) to more dynamic (one breath in each position) to setting rest intervals between 500- or 1000-meter repeats on my rowing machine.

Purposeful Exaggeration

When I coached age-group swimmers I had this experience many times: I'd spot a swimmer needing a stroke correction; for instance, doing backstroke with an entry far behind her head. I'd stop the swimmer, let her know she was over-reaching on entry and ask her to slice her hand in outside her ear. She would push off and gamely try to make the correction, usually moving her hand about a quarter of an inch to the side, when I'd been hoping for a shift of four or five inches. So I'd then instruct her to enter *way outside* her shoulder. That would usually bring the desired result — the hand entering just outside the ear.

This shows how stubborn habits can be. There is only one way to permanently correct an error of this sort: thousands of correct repetitions...and strictly avoiding any more incorrect reps. And the surest way to accelerate the correction process is to over-compensate for the old way.

For that reason, there are elements of "purposeful exaggeration" in most TI drills. Rotating to Sweet Spot allows you to practice body-roll in a far wider range than you'll need in whole-stroke swimming. This over-corrects for the common "human swimming" tendency to swim too flat. Switching "too far" in the Under-Switch drill corrects the tendency to finish the switch short of the Sweet Spot. Practicing stroke recovery with the hand under water, as we'll do in the Zipper-Switch series over-corrects for the common error of swinging the recovery arm too wide and high. Practicing FQS (Front-Quadrant Swimming) switches with extra overlap or catch-up over-corrects for the common tendency toward "rear-quadrant" stroke timing.

Purposeful exaggeration works just as well in whole-strokeswimming too. Super-slow swimming allows exaggerated practice of leisurely, complete arm extension before stroking, of super-low stroke counts, and of silent swimming, all of which will help accelerate correction of old habits of choppy, hurried, splashy strokes common among virtually every swimmer on earth.

Lesson One: Finding Balance and Your "Sweet Spot"

This is the "ridiculously simple" part of *martial arts swimming*, at least for some athletes. If you consider yourself a pretty fair swimmer already, if you've done countless hard training repeats, or finished the swim leg of several races in fairly good position, you may be tempted to skip this part of the progression. Don't! If you have human DNA — even if you've already swum in the Olympics — you can still improve your balance, and as it improves you'll use less energy at any speed.

If, on the other hand, every stroke you've ever taken has been a frustrating struggle, if you're "toast" after two laps, if you always feel as if your toenails are in danger of scraping the pool bottom, this lesson can be transforming. Lesson One has the potential of giving you an unprecedented feeling of being supported by the water, of basically being able to *just lie there*, kicking gently, while tension and discomfort melt away. Once you have that, you'll immediately swim with far more ease, and the rest of the lessons will go much more smoothly.

Head First?

In watching underwater video of thousands of "human swimmers" over the years, what I notice first is how completely their hands and arms are occupied with *trying not to sink*. They may think what they're doing is "stroking" but virtually none of their energy is producing propulsion; most of it goes into fighting "that sinking feeling." Until you learn to balance effortlessly without your arms helping, it is simply impossible to drill or stroke efficiently. Thus your first step in learning should be to get the water to support you without help from your arms. In these "head-lead" drills, because you're unable to use your arms for support, you'll learn to balance your body entirely through proper head position and weight distribution.

What about Fins?

A fair proportion of the triathlete population — most of those who were runners first — are the sort who go backwards when using a kick-board, because of inflexible ankles. If that's you, fins can be a great aid in parts of the drill sequence, but it's best to do Lesson One without them, at least at first. The point of this lesson is to balance using your head and torso, but the temptation to use fins may be great. If you find yourself reasonably balanced but looking up at the same ceiling tile for a long time, just stand up, relax a moment, then push off the bottom to give yourself some momentum. It's much easier to maintain momentum while moving, than to generate it once you've lost it. And don't respond to a slow or non-propulsive kick by kicking harder. Becoming a faster kicker is not the point; instead, keep your kick compact and gentle and make it your goal to use less effort, not more. Continued drill practice, combined with some vertical kicking and judicious use of fins will gradually make your uncooperative kick effective enough to sustain smooth, relaxed drilling.

Stand taller by pressing your hand higher

Four Simple Secrets to Success

1.   As you practice, imagine being towed by a line attached to the top of your head. Keep your head-spine line long and straight. Rehearse on deck by standing and placing one hand on top of your head. Remain flat-footed and try to stand taller by pressing your hand a quarter of an inch higher. Take your hand away and memorize the sensation of a long, straight, head-spine line. Refer to that sensation occasionally during Lesson One.

2. Practice **ease**. Move as quietly and economically as you can, trying not to disturb the water. Strive for an almost Zen-like sensation of stillness.

3. Kick silently and gently with a long, straight, supple leg. Keep your feet inside your body's wake or "shadow." If you feel slow, don't kick harder; instead, try to reduce resistance by improving your balance and alignment.

4. Most important, when practicing Lesson One for the first time, use a short, shallow pool section, where you can stand up at any time. You move slowly when doing head-lead drills, and with a weak kick even 25 yards can be tiring. Until you can do just 10 yards effortlessly, don't go farther. (Backyard and motel pools are often perfect for Lesson One practice!) If you feel tired or are working too hard, don't push on. Instead, stand up, take a few deep breaths, and relax before resuming.

Drill #1: Basic Balance on Your Back

Why we do it: This is the easiest way to relax and enjoy the support of the water. You don't have to worry about breathing, so you can just lie there and experience balance. *Effortlessness and stability* are the key sensations of balance; learn them here then maintain in other positions.

Follow this sequence (kicking gently at each step):

1. Hide your head. Get comfortable with a new head position. Water should wet the top of your forehead, the bottom of your chin, and the corners of your goggles. Your face should be parallel to the surface. Resist the temptation to raise your chin to create a "safe breathing space." Tuck it slightly to keep your head aligned. If other swimmers splash waves in your face, you can minimize this distraction by wearing nose-clips. Spend 5 to 10 minutes simply getting your head position right or have a partner check the picture and help. Patiently practice until it feels more natural and you're comfortable with the water that close. **In every subsequent drill, hide your head before doing anything else.**

Water should wet the corners of your goggles.

2. Make a "hull shape" with your back. It's harder to balance with your shoulders back and your chest thrust forward. Round your shoulders slightly and shape your back like the hull of a boat. Use this position for all balance drills.

3. Press your "buoy." In simple terms, you achieve balance by "lying on your lungs" which are the most buoyant part of your body. Keeping your head hidden and torso hull-shaped, lean on your upper back until your hips feel light. When you're balanced, you'll show a "dry patch of thigh" on each kick. But don't let your kick become splashy; your knees and toes should just ruffle the surface. In subsequent drills, keep your "buoy" pressed in the same way.

4. Just lie there. The true test of balance is being able to *do nothing* with your arms. If you need to brace yourself or scull with them, you aren't balanced. When you are really supported by the water, you can use your arms just to help shape yourself into a torpedo.

5. Time to practice. Limit repeats to 25 yards or less. As soon as you begin losing your sense of ease and relaxation, rest until you regain it. Focus mainly on the sense of stillness produced when you can just lie there, kicking gently, and let the water do the work. Imagine being so stable that you could carry a champagne glass on your forehead. *This feeling is a hallmark of balance!* Keep it as you progress to other balance drills.

Use a noodle to relax and kick gently.

Special Help for "Sinkers"

Athletes who are lean, densely muscled or long-legged (and particularly those with two or more of these traits) commonly find that no amount of head-hiding and buoy-pressing allows them to be as effortlessly supported as others. Rather than struggle to float those "heavy" legs, use one of the foam "noodles" found at most pools. Rest your lower back in the center and lie back with your head hidden and upper back pressed in and your arms inside the noodle. The noodle's support can help you learn to kick more gently and efficiently since your legs won't be reacting to that sinking feeling. Practice for a while, to see how your torso and legs behave when fully supported. You have two choices for the next step. Try both:

• **Lose your noodle.** After moving gently along for 10 yards or so, gradually move the noodle to your knees and continue kicking in balance for a similar distance. Finally release it altogether. Repeat until you feel nearly the same without the noodle as with it.

• **Roll a bit.** Keep the noodle in place as you try the slight rotation of Drill #2. The point isn't to rely on the noodle forever, but to use it to let you know how effortless support will feel, then use that kinesthetic "cue" as your guide to balancing with less reliance on the noodle.

Drill #2: Find Your "Sweet Spot"

Why we do it: You'll swim mainly on your side and start and finish every drill on your side, but "side balance" is almost never exactly on the side. The "Sweet Spot" is where you'll find true equilibrium and balance and is influenced by your body type. If you're lean or densely muscled, side balance will probably be almost on your back. Finding your Sweet Spot is critical because you'll start and finish every drill here. When you master Sweet Spot, you'll drill with ease and fluency; if you don't take time to master it, you'll struggle instead.

Follow this sequence:

1. Start as in Drill #1, palms at your side. Remain on your back until you check your head position and feel effortlessly balanced.

2. Without moving your head, roll *just enough* for the knuckles of one hand to barely clear the water. Your goal is to find a position where one arm is dry from shoulder to knuckles and you're just as comfortable as you were on your back. If you feel any discomfort, return to your back and try again with less rotation.

3. Check that your head is still positioned as in Drill #1, with the water at the corners of your goggles.

4. Watch for signs of discomfort: lifting the head, craning the neck, arching your back, helping with your lower arm. If you feel any tension, return to your back and start over with less rotation.

Roll just enough for one hand to clear the water

5. Once you feel at home in Sweet Spot, focus on **staying tall and slipping through a small hole in the water**, then on making stillness, quiet, and effortlessness feel natural.

6. Repeat on your other side. You may feel more comfortable on one side than the other. I call this having a "chocolate" (better balance) and "vanilla" side. Balance improvements on your vanilla side will usually bring greater dividends. Alternate one length or minute on one side with a similar distance or time on the other side.

7. When you begin to feel comfortable on each side, begin practicing Active Balance. Kick easily on one side for three yoga breaths, then roll gently to show the other arm for three breaths. The two key skills in Active Balance are 1) maintain constant equilibrium as you roll and 2) use effortless weight shifts to initiate body roll. Roll *without using your arms*, without kicking harder, and without disturbing the water. Keep your head in a steady position, with water at the corners of your goggles as you roll from side to side, as if carrying a champagne glass on your forehead.

Lesson One Practice Plan

1. Give yourself unlimited time to acquire effortless ease. *You are not on a schedule to advance to Lesson Two.* Your primary goals are to make the "hidden" head position a habit, to make the feeling of being supported by the water natural and to allow your vanilla side to feel as comfortable as your chocolate side.

2. When drilling for an extended period (25 yards or a minute) on one side, use the champagne glass image again, but this time imagine that you are also carrying it on the exposed shoulder.

3. A comprehensive series for Lesson One practice is 25 yards on your back, 25 on your right side, 25 on your left, and 25 of Active Balance. Rest for three to five yoga breaths after each 25. As your Sweet Spot balance improves, you can do Drill #1 less often, focusing your practice on side balance and active balance. As you progress to other drills, a 5- to 10-minute tune-up of Lesson One practice before tackling more advanced drills will always be beneficial.

The Skiing Lesson

Brent Jordan posted the following at a TI online discussion: "I'm a life-long cyclist and have just started training for triathlons. This is my first experience in swimming. I have done swimming drills from the video twice a week for about a month but can still do only 50 yards before having to stop and rest. My question is: Am I just experiencing a lack of swimming endurance, or should I be able to swim farther without resting by now?"

Recently I was at a similar place as a cross-country skier, at least in the freestyle method (also known as skating). I've been skiing classic style for 10 years, which, in my case, seems almost an impediment to learning the skating style. I've got too much muscle memory for classic cross-country. Perhaps I'd learn skating faster with a completely blank slate.

In February 2001, after devoting a few days each winter since 1998 to skating on rented skis, I finally bought my own set and drove to Lake Placid for a long weekend of learning. On Friday morning, everything I had painstakingly learned in previous winters was forgotten as I scrabbled helplessly around the flat stadium area at the site of the 1980 Olympic races. But then I recalled the initial drill from my first skating lesson three years earlier: Take your left ski off, place your right (ski-shod) foot in one of the tracks cut for classic skiers and, using your left (ski-less) foot, push off and glide. The stadium field is about 150 yards long; I figured that two trips (300 yards) of balance practice on each foot should give me a sufficient foundation to progress to the next drill.

Off I went...but for only 30 yards before exhaustion set in. I took inventory: My skiing foot and shin were burning because I seemed to be clenching it tightly, rather than just "riding the ski." And everything else seemed to be working far too hard because my body went too far past the balance point (directly over the ski) every time I pushed off, forcing me to use sheer effort to haul my 200+ pounds back to the centerline. And because shaky balance forced me to put my pushing foot down so quickly, I got no glide, making my movements choppy and rushed. Was I exhausted because I lacked "skiing endurance?" Definitely not. My problem was massive amounts of wasted energy, not lack of energy.

"Okay, time to regroup," I thought. Starting again, but more deliberately and slowly, I went a bit farther before needing rest. I finally made it the full 150 yards, in four intervals with rest periods between. Heading back, I made it in three stages. I was feeling my foot relax and my body was beginning to figure out how to balance right over the ski then glide a bit with the pushing foot raised. As my balance improved, I also found myself able to add power to my pushoff.

I switched the ski to my left foot for the next trip down and back: Time to figure out balance with the other side of my body (and brain). I also made a mental shift. Rather than plan on a certain number of trips, I decided to just keep practicing the balance drill, at least until I could make 150 yards non-stop on each foot. As it happens it took about 10 total trips (nearly a mile of practice) to complete a nonstop lap on each leg.

I might have moved on to another drill then, but I decided to continue practicing basic balance for a while longer, wanting to do it beyond relaxation and ease — almost to the point of boredom. Not the boredom of lack of engagement, but the kind where your body falls into such an effortless flow that it can carry on without much conscious oversight from your brain. It was a wise decision. I used the "do it till' you're bored" philosophy for a series of five other drills over the next four hours before doing just a bit of whole-skill practice — skiing without poles around the flat stadium field at the end of the day. And when I finally left the stadium to try a loop of a gently rolling, 1.5-kilometer beginner's course the next day, I stopped for rest (5 to 10 yoga breaths) whenever I felt the slightest fatigue or inefficiency. The result? I made really exciting progress during 10 cumulative hours of practice over the 3-day weekend.

The lesson for Brent and anyone else hoping to learn fluent Fishlike swimming is the same as I learned while skiing:
1. Start with the simplest balance drill — Lesson One, Drill #1.
2. Practice it with no set time limit or number of repetitions in mind.
3. Stay with it until it becomes effortless.
4. Then continue a bit longer until you are "bored" (you can do it without mental effort).

5. Only then should you progress to the next drill or skill.

6. Make a commitment to avoid "practicing struggle" at any stage. Any time you feel yourself losing control or edging toward fatigue, stop and rest, regroup at the prior drill or skill, or do both.

If you don't, you'll simply end up imprinting struggle in your muscle memory and your body will naturally revert to inefficient patterns whenever you get a little bit tired.

Lesson Two: Becoming Weightless and Slippery

After using head-lead drills in Lesson One to become effortlessly horizontal — and freeing your arms from helping with balance — we can now extend a "weightless arm" to make your "vessel" more slippery. As we explained in Chapter 6, when your bodyline becomes longer, drag is reduced, allowing you to swim faster without working harder. This lesson will give you a balanced vessel that is longer and more slippery.

Three Simple Secrets to Success

1. As you extend your bodyline from your outstretched hand to your toes, it's important to keep that line as long, straight, and sleek as possible, but don't over-stretch to the point of tension.

2. Any time you feel uncomfortable or unbalanced — or feel the need to use your arm for support — (not uncommon when doing Lesson Two for the first time), return your extended arm to your side and re-balance in Head-Lead Sweet Spot.

3. Just as we encourage students to master Lesson One without fins, we also encourage them to feel free to use fins to increase their ease in Lesson Two. If you are balanced (completely supported by the water, top arm dry) but still have to kick too hard, you can benefit from using fins. The ease they provide allows you to reduce tension in your whole body, to reduce fatigue and save energy for refinement. Developing a stronger kick is unimportant; a more economical movement style is all-important.

Drill #3: Hand-Lead Sweet Spot — Lengthen Your "Vessel"

Why we do it: To experience how balance feels with an arm extended and to imprint your most *slippery* body position. Hand-Lead Sweet Spot is also the position in which you'll start and finish every drill. Finally, it's one of the two best positions for practicing flutter kick. (Skating Position — Drill #4 — is the other.)

Follow this sequence:

1. Start as in Drill #1, balanced on your back. Is the water at the corners of your goggles? Do you feel effortlessly supported? (Take all the time you need to feel this.) Then roll just enough to show one arm. Do you still feel comfortable? Do you have a long, clean head-spine line? Is your top arm dry from shoulder to knuckles? If not, return to your back and start over. If yes, then....

2. "Sneak" your lower arm to full extension. *Your hand should be an inch or two below the surface.* Your palm can be up, down, or sideways. Your arm should feel as if it's just floating forward.

3. Next, make yourself needle-like. Once your arm is extended and weightless, check the gap between the back of your head and your shoulder. Narrow the gap if possible, *but avoid strain or discomfort.* Finally, make sure your head is aligned with your spine with water at the corners of both goggles, and that your top arm lies easily on your side with a dry strip of skin from shoulder to knuckles.

4. Practice until you could glide blissfully in this position on either side indefinitely. Take the time to make your "vanilla" side feel as good as your "chocolate" side; patience here will pay big dividends later.

How to practice: Once you feel "bliss" on either side, practice 1-length repeats (resting for 3 or more yoga breaths between) for 7 to 10 minutes, alternating sides. Choose one of these focal points for each length:

1. Create a long clean line from extended fingertips to toes.

2. Slip through the smallest possible hole in the water. Make sure your head slips through the same "hole" that your body is traveling through.

3. Glide silently and effortlessly. Kick gently, keeping your legs long, supple, and within the "shadow" of your body. (Use fins if this is impossible.)

4. If at any time you lose balance or comfort, put your arm back to your side and start over.

Drill #4: Balance in the Skating Position

Why we do it: This is your first opportunity to experience balance as it should feel when you begin swimming. This is also the first movement in all the Switch drills that follow. Last, but not least, this is the first drill in which you practice the proper technique for breathing, developing good habits now, that you can maintain right through to whole-stroke. Here you'll learn to breathe by rolling your body to where the air is — rather than lifting or turning your head. The act of rolling your body to breathe imprints the critical habit (when drilling) of *finishing every rolling movement in Sweet Spot.*

Follow this sequence:

1. Start as in Drill #3. Balance on your back and hide your head, then roll gently to show one arm, and finally extend the other arm. Allow each position to feel *great* before you move to the next.

2. After sneaking your arm up, pause to check: Is the water still at the corners of both goggles? Do you feel like a long, balanced needle slipping through a small hole? Is your top arm dry? Then...

3. Swivel your head and look directly at the bottom. After you look down, pause and check: Is your head hidden and aligned; are you balanced on your side with your extended hand below your head; do you feel great balance — even a downhill gliding sensation?

4. Stay for a comfortable interval, then roll *all the way back to where you started*. At first, most of our students need to roll "too far" in order to breathe comfortably. If you feel unbalanced or uncomfortable after you roll up to breathe, you haven't rolled far enough. If you feel quite comfortable, you have.

5. Stay in Sweet Spot for at least three yoga breaths before rolling nose-down again; avoid feeling breathless or rushed.

Lesson Two Practice Plan

Let's review what you've learned so far. Balance and head-spine alignment in Lesson One. How to make yourself more slippery (reducing *wave drag* by lengthening your bodyline and *form drag* by making yourself needle-like). How balance should feel when you begin swimming. And finally, how to breathe while rolling your needle shape to where the air is. These insights will all be of extraordinary value in making you a more Fishlike swimmer, so you should make extensive use of Lesson Two drills in refining your stroke, even after it has become quite efficient. So there is almost immeasurable benefit in taking time now to patiently polish all the fine points.

As with Lesson One, there's a simple 100-yard sequence for practicing Lesson Two skills: 50 yards of Drill 3 (25 on your right side; 25 on your left) plus 50 yards in the Skating position (25 right, 25 left). Rest for 3 or more "yoga" breaths after each length and practice for 7 to 10 minutes. Choose a focal point for each length. For Drill 3, choose from among those mentioned. For the Skating position, choose from among the following:

1. Head Position. Keep your head right in line with your body at all times. Water at the corners of your goggles while looking up. Nose pointed directly at the bottom while looking down with your head positioned so water can easily flow over the back. Head tucked against the extended arm as you roll from one position to the other.

2. Balance. Particularly when nose-down, focus on feeling completely supported by the water, almost as if you're sliding downhill. To get this, make sure your head is hidden, that your hand is below your head, and that you lean on your lungs.

3. *Really* balanced. You'll know you've reached this state when you can glide effortlessly — almost lazily — watching pool tiles slide by underneath you.

4. Slippery. We call this the Skating Position because the sensation should be of using the extended side of your body — from fingertips to toes — as if it was a skate blade. Being able to balance right on your side — shoulder pointed straight up — is the most slippery position you can achieve in the water. Enhance this by slipping your body through the smallest possible space in the water, to minimize form drag on body surfaces.

5. Breathing. Maintain your needle shape as you swivel and roll nose-down to the Skating Position — and particularly as you roll "too far" when you swivel back to Sweet Spot to breathe.

Lesson Three: Tapping Effortless Power from Your Kinetic Chain

The first two lessons have taught you balance and slippery body positions. In Lesson Three, you will learn to use rotation of your balanced and slippery core body to generate effortless power for propulsion. Lesson Three also introduces you to the first of our three Switch drill sequences. These will be the most dynamic and powerful movements you have yet practiced.

Drill #5: Under Skate

Why we do it: You learned the most valuable form of balance in the Skating position. That position becomes the basis for other ways of practicing balance with a different dynamic. This drill is really a mini drill — a rehearsal for Drill #6: Under Switch. It also reinforces the key skills of staying on your side as you swim, and of rolling a balanced, aligned, slippery body to breathe. It further imprints the habit of *finishing all rolling motions in Sweet Spot.*

Follow this sequence:

1. Begin as in Drill #4, moving deliberately and patiently through all four positions or movements practiced previously: Balance on your back; then rotate slightly to Sweet Spot, showing an arm, then sneak your other arm to full extension; and finally swivel down to the Skating Position.

2. After you look down, pause and check: Are you looking down with your head hidden and aligned; are you balanced on your side with your extended hand below your head; do you feel great balance — even a downhill gliding sensation?

3. If so, then sneak the trailing hand forward *under water* (wipe it across your belly and past your jaw) until you see the hand right under your nose. Check that you're still on your side with your shoulders stacked, then slide the hand back to your side. Finish by rolling your needle shape *all the way back to Sweet Spot.*

4. Take at least three yoga breaths, then repeat the sequence. You'll probably fit in three cycles in each 25 yards. Switch sides on the next length.

How to practice: Your key focal points are the same as for Drill #4, but with added emphasis on remaining *on your side* as you bring your hand to your face, and on slipping through the smallest hole in the water as you do it. Practice Under Skate by itself, alternating sides. Or practice it in a series with Lesson Two drills: 50 yards each (25 right, 25 left) of Drills 2, 3, 4, and 5. Some athletes can master this drill after no more than 10 minutes of practice. If you feel you've got it, move on. If not, spend as much time as you need because the skills learned in Under Skate are key to every drill that follows.

Drill #6: Under Switch

Why we do it: This is the first drill to tap the power of the kinetic chain by teaching you how to link an armstroke to core-body rotation for effortless propulsion. It also simplifies the learning process for learning the front-quadrant stroke timing that keeps your bodyline long, by giving you a visual cue for when to make the switch.

Follow this sequence:

1. After the movements of Under Skate seem natural (almost a "no-brainer"), you can move easily to the full drill. Start as in Drill #5, but when you see your hand under your nose, keep moving it forward to full extension as you roll (switch) to Sweet Spot on the other side.

2. Take at least three yoga breaths (relax, normalize your breathing, and get your bearings) as you check your balance and make sure that you *are* in Sweet Spot again. Then, swivel to Nose Down/90...pause...and repeat in the other direction.

3. The basic movements are simple, but the opportunities for refinement are many. Practice these focal points, one at a time:

• Be patient. Don't switch until you see your hand under your nose.

• Finish the switch in your Sweet Spot. When first learning this drill, most of our workshop students need to exaggerate and roll (switch) *too far* in order to finish in Sweet Spot.

• Another way to reinforce this is to switch as if you were planning to breathe with your belly button. After you see your hand, take your belly button to the air; your head just goes along for the ride.

• Stay connected as you switch: When you see your hand, move arm, head, and torso as a unit.

• Stay slippery: Switch through the smallest possible hole in the water.

• Once you have the parts working smoothly together, focus on doing the drill as quietly as possible. This will help you do any drill more fluently and economically.

• Final step: Pause your kick at the moment you see your hand and switch. Resume gentle kicking once you're back in Sweet Spot. (See box on page 96 following this lesson for more details.)

Drill #7: Double Under Switch

Why we do it: Switch drills teach powerful, coordinated, effortless movement of the core body. Multi-switch (2 or more switches) drills introduce swimming rhythms (steady, rhythmic core-body rotation) to these movements, but retain pauses in the Sweet Spot, to allow time to regroup, evaluate your practice, and make fine adjustments.

Follow this sequence:

1. Start as in Drill #6 but do two Switches before pausing in Sweet Spot again.

2. After you roll to the Skating position, pause to check your balance. Lean in to feel the support of the water, then sneak your hand forward.

3. Wait to see your hand before both switches. Keep your head "hidden" and look directly at the bottom through both switches.

4. Finish in Sweet Spot and breathe three times before rolling to nose-down again.

5. Start the next length on your other side: Look down…see your hand…Switch…glide a bit…see your hand…Switch…Breathe in your Sweet Spot.

6. Practice until you feel yourself gliding effortlessly in balance…and until your Switch timing is consistent.

Drill #8: Triple Under Switch

Why we do it: This drill will give you even more space to make yourself more Fishlike and learn the feel of a swimming rhythm.

Follow this sequence:

Just add one switch to the previous drill. Use the extra rhythm time to feel all of the following:

• Keep your head hidden. Water should flow over the back of your head during all three switches.

• Keep your timing consistent. Switch at the exact moment you see your hand under your nose.

• Extend both hands fully, front and back, then glide just a moment before recovering for the next switch.

- During your glide, feel yourself just lying there supported by the water. That's the feeling of great balance.
- Maintain a focus on piercing the water, particularly while sneaking your arm and switching.
- When all of that begins to feel somewhat natural, see if you can pause your kick during the three switches….Pick it up again in Sweet Spot.
- Finally reduce the glide between switches. Roll your body a bit less during the three switches, to increase rhythm.

Lesson Three Practice Plan

The movements and coordination were relatively simple in the first two lessons. Lesson Three involves more complex movements, though we've presented them in a way designed to ease your learning curve. More complexity brings more opportunity for confusion. Simplify by doing two things: 1) Allow more practice time for Lesson Three before advancing to Lesson Four and 2) spend a bit more time on focused practice of each of the Lesson Three drills by themselves before combining them in the sequences suggested below.

Here are some suggested sequences (always warm up with at least 10 minutes refresher practice of Drills 2, 3, and 4).

- 200-yard repeats: 50 yards each (25 right, 25 left) of Drills 2, 3, 4, and 5.
- 100-yard repeats: 25 Under Skate on your right side, 25 Under Switch, 25 Under Skate left, 25 Under Switch.
- 150-yard repeats: 50 Under Skate (25 right, 25 left), 50 Under Switch, 50 Double Under Switch (25 balance on right, 25 on left).
- 150-yard repeats: 25 Under Skate right, 25 Under Switch, 25 Double Under Switch right + 25 Under Skate left, 25 Under Switch, 25 Double Under Switch left.

Until you have put in a cumulative total of several hours practice in Lesson Three drills, rest for at least 3 yoga breaths after each length. Similarly, take three yoga breaths or bobs in your Sweet Spot between cycles of each drill.

Let Go of Your Kick: How to Make an Economical, Relaxed, 2-Beat Your Natural Kick

Most triathletes kick too much. It's not that they want to; they can't help it. Because they aren't balanced, they feel their legs sinking and react by kicking more. This kicking is not only ineffective (i.e., not even slightly propulsive) and energy-wasting, but also wrecks their rhythm and any chance of achieving fluency.

The ideal kick for most people — i.e., anyone not trying to swim fast for a short distance (under 200 meters) — is one that is non-overt. That doesn't mean passive, exactly, but nearly effortless. This is particularly true if, after finishing your swim, you need to cycle for an hour or more and then go running. It's far better to save those leg muscles for when you *must* use them.

Non-overt kicking should be fairly easy for you when wearing a wetsuit; after all, the neoprene body-wrap makes your legs so buoyant it should be easy to let them float behind, while you swim. Unfortunately, all the muscle memory built up during your training (*not* wearing a wetsuit) is still there, as is the rest of the ragged swimming style caused by the leg-churning you've spent so many hours practicing.

Your drills are the perfect device for helping you shed that energy-wasting kick and replace it with an economical kick — the kind that mainly helps your body roll from side to side more crisply. This is called a 2-beat kick (for two kicks in each stroke cycle). Yes, there is some overt kicking going on as you drill. This is because while you're paused in Sweet Spot between drill cycles you need to maintain momentum. But when your body — particularly the kinetic chain — is providing momentum, you should let your legs take a rest. You can train them for this in two ways.

Let Fins Do the Work

If you're the type of swimmer who goes nowhere fast — and perhaps moves *backwards* — when using a kickboard, you're also likely to work too hard at kicking during the less dynamic parts of drill practice — simple balance drills in Lessons One and Two and whenever you're in Sweet Spot in Lessons Three to Five. You do this mainly because your ankles are inflexible and non-propulsive, often from countless miles of running. Because your ankles don't flex, your knees flex instead and you end up with a running-style motion that pushes a lot of water around and creates lots of turbulence, but little forward motion.

While a steady kick is required during the Sweet Spot pause (because a body in motion tends to remain in motion, while a body that's come to rest is hard to get moving again on the next drill cycle), you don't want that kick sucking up a lot of energy. You want it be nearly effortless, and with your rigid ankles that's nearly impossible. The solution, particularly as you learn the drills, is to let fins do the work. You move your legs as easily as possible; the fin blade takes care of the flexion your ankles refuse to do, and you move along nicely. With kicking no longer a source of fatigue, you can put more of your energy into fine-motor control and can practice longer with the energy to do it well. You also begin to lose the habit of over-kicking.

Let Your Body Do the Work

The second part of this leg-saving equation is to use Switch drills to learn the timing of the 2-beat kick. This kick does a wonderfully efficient job of helping the body roll from side to side, which generates ample power for propulsion. You can swim with this kick virtually all day without tiring. When you do this right, you should be able to swim any distance and still mount your bicycle with fresh legs.

The mechanism for learning is fairly simple. Whenever you do any of the switch drills — Under Switch, Zipper Switch, or Over Switch — practice letting your legs go just as you make the switch. Pause them for an instant, and when you return to Sweet Spot, resume gentle, steady kicking. Keep kicking easily as you swivel to the nose-down position, but as your hand slices in to initiate the switch, pause your kick and let your body glide forward on the momentum from your weight shift and body rotation. After you rebalance in Sweet Spot, pick up the kick again.

It's the same with the Multi-Switch versions of all three drills. When practicing Double- or Triple-Under, keep your head in line with your spine and lean on your chest until you feel supported by the water. That sense of being able to just lie there during your three switches frees you to let your legs become more passive. Now you're ready to use Multi Switch practice to teach yourself a relaxed, economical, 2-beat kick. As in the single-switch drills, maintain a gentle kick while in Sweet Spot and when you swivel to the Skating Position, but once your hand slices in on the first switch, let your legs pause. They won't actually remain motionless. Instead one leg should beat down as each hand enters the water. As your right hand enters, your left leg kicks; as your left hand enters, your right leg kicks.

Don't use too many brain cells *trying* to coordinate this. Instead, focus on letting the legs do what comes naturally when you just pause the steady kick you'd been using prior to the switch. Your arms and legs already are well acquainted with moving in a counter-balancing fashion. Running or walking, they do the same: Right arm and left leg swing forward together, then left arm and right leg.

When to Practice "Letting Go"
Each lesson includes a practice plan. Make kick coordination the final thing you polish in each lesson. The first step is to learn and imprint proper head position, balance, switch timing, etc. It will be much easier to let go of your kick once you've mastered these key skills. Once you've learned the knack of "letting go" in Under Switch and Double Under (Drills 6 and 7), it should be much easier to do the same thing in the Zipper series (Drills 10. 11, and 12) and Over Switches that follow it. To integrate a 2-beat kick into your whole-stroke swimming, alternate a length of multi-switch drilling with a length of swimming, focusing mainly on having your kick feel the same in each. By the time you squeeze into your wetsuit for a race, a passive kick should feel like the most natural thing in the world. Your legs will thank you profusely when you begin pedaling and running.

Lesson Four: Mastering a Compact, Relaxed Recovery

Having mastered Lesson Three, you should now have experienced two important elements of Fishlike Swimming: First, how to generate effortless propulsion by using your hand to simply hold on to a spot in the water while dynamic body-roll takes you past that spot. Second, how to keep your bodyline long and to "lie on your lungs" while doing that rhythmically. Our next step will give you an even stronger sense of balance and start imprinting the muscle memory for a compact, relaxed recovery. Having painstakingly developed a balanced, aligned foundation for stroking, we don't want to let an arm-swinging recovery upset that. This lesson teaches you an energy-saving, alignment-preserving, drag-reducing recovery.

Drill #9: Zipper Skate

Why we do it: We used Under Skate (Drill #5) as kinesthetic rehearsal for Under Switch (Drill #6) and to practice a slightly more dynamic form of balance. Zipper Skate serves exactly the same purpose in preparing for Zipper Switch. But it can be even more valuable in preparing you for whole-stroke swimming because it's the ideal way to gain the most powerful sense of where your balance point (your "buoy") is. Once you know that balance point *in your bones*, you'll know how to have a truly relaxed, unhurried recovery and stroke.

Follow this sequence:
1. Begin as in Drill #5. When you arrive at the Skating Position, rather than recover under water, drag your hand slowly along your side (as if pulling up a zipper). Keep your hand under the surface, as shown in the photo.
2. Lead with your elbow for as long as possible, with your hand trailing until elbow and hand are alongside your ear. (Tip: It can be extremely helpful to practice this movement while lying on your side on the pool deck or on your floor at home — see photo on the next page.)
3. Once your arm is in the "shark-fin" position, briefly check that your shoulders are still stacked, then slide your hand back down. Finish by rolling your needle shape *all the way back to Sweet Spot*. Take 3 cleansing breaths, then repeat.

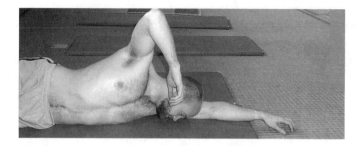

Practice Zipper Skate on dry land first. Lie in Skating Position, nose down. Leading with your elbow, drag your hand along your rib cage until its hanging alongside your ear. Your elbow pointing up and your arm relaxed. Then slide it back.

How to practice: Over time this will probably be your most valuable balance drill and the one you should practice most often. It will give you a clear picture of a) how well you've mastered balance, b) where your supporting "buoy" is, and c) how to use that awareness to steadily improve your balance. After you've learned the basic movements (particularly the elbow leading the hand, and the hand remaining under water), I recommend you use the practice-till-you're-bored philosophy to fully develop your kinesthetic balance awareness and burn it into your nervous system. You could easily practice this drill non-stop for 15 to 30 minutes once a week for the next month or two and learn valuable lessons on every lap. Here are a few focal points:

1. Are you stable or do you immediately begin to sink as your arm comes forward? If you begin to sink right away, make sure you keep your weight forward and the extended arm below your head. Your goal — if you sink — is to sink in a horizontal position with your armpit at the same level as your hips and feet. This is enormously valuable to learning equilibrium. If you're a sinker, bring your hand to your shoulder and *immediately* slide it back to your side.

2. If your body position remains fairly stable as you draw your arm forward, "skate" for a few seconds with your elbow motionless above your shoulder. The weight of your arm in the air should give you a clear sense of how to balance by "lying on your lungs." If you feel balanced while doing this, practice doing the recovery super slowly. This is the nearest sensation thus far of how you'd like to feel once you begin wholestroke swimming.

3. Focus on sensing the water resistance against your hand on recovery. Don't fight it. Instead yield to the resistance by softening your hand and arm. How compact and gentle can you make that recovery action?

4. If you're in the "sinkers" group on this drill, fins will allow you to sense the stable support a balanced swimmer feels when doing this drill.

Drill #10: Zipper Switch

Why we do it: The compact, relaxed, unhurried recovery you are learning will be an important key to effectively linking your armstroke to the power of core-body rotation. This drill will also teach you the front-quadrant timing that keeps your bodyline long throughout the stroke cycle. The purposeful exaggeration on this drill is to slice your hand in alongside your ear, before slicing it forward underwater. This corrects the nearly universal tendency to over-reach on the recovery.

Follow this sequence:
1. Begin as in Drill #9. Move deliberately from Sweet Spot to the Skating position, then check that you are balanced — feeling great support — with your extended hand below your head.

2. Do a "Zipper" recovery with your hand under water, elbow leading as far forward as possible. Feel water resistance on your hand, but don't fight it. Soften your arm and hand and keep them close to shoulder and ear.

3. As soon as your hand catches up to the elbow, slice it *in and forward* as you switch and roll to Sweet Spot on the other side.

4. Relax and glide in Sweet Spot for as long as you want (3 yoga breaths), then repeat in the other direction. As you practice, emphasize the following:

• A compact and unhurried recovery. Continue to focus on switching through the smallest possible space, but that space is now above and below the surface.

• **Hand entry that is exaggeratedly early and close to your head.** Drive your hand into the water alongside your ear to over-correct the tendency to over-reach.

• Practice silently, taking all the time you need to feel "in your bones" the right moment in your recovery to make the switch.

• Continue to feel "connected" to your core-body as you switch.

Drill #11: Double Zipper Switch

Why we do it: As in Double Under Switch, Double Zipper introduces swimming rhythms to the movements you've just learned. You're coming ever closer to actual swimming.

Follow this sequence:

Start as in Zipper Switch, but do two Switches before pausing in Sweet Spot again.

1. After you roll to the Skating position, check your balance. Feel the water supporting you, then draw your hand forward. Feel the water resisting your hand at all times.

2. Switch when your hand is alongside your ear.

3. Keep your head "hidden" and look directly at the bottom through both switches.

4. Finish in Sweet Spot and take three breaths before rolling nose-down again.

5. Start the next length on your other side.

Drill #12: Triple Zipper Switch

Why we do it: We're right on the verge of whole-stroke swimming. Doing more Zipper Switches primes you to transition from skillful drilling to beautiful swimming. Give your student the freedom to do as many switches as they feel comfortable doing. The most relaxed and rhythmic students can do as many as six before needing to return to Sweet Spot to breathe.

Follow this sequence:

1. When you feel good balance and timing and have an unhurried, relaxed recovery, progress to Triple Zipper. Focus on the same points as in Triple Under: head hidden, steady unhurried core-body rhythm, consistent "switch" timing. Here are some specific instructions you can give:

• **Hide your head...** Water should flow over the back of your head much of the time... Look straight down and watch yourself slide effortlessly past tiles on the pool bottom.

• **Hug the Water...** *Hug* the surface, as if you were swimming under a very low ceiling.

- ***Pierce* the water...** Slip through the smallest possible space both above and below the surface.
- **Soften your arms and hands...** Feel the water resist your hand, but try to recover without splash or turbulence.
- **Feel the complete support of the water** and use it to bring your hand forward as slowly as you can.
- **And finally drill without making a sound.**

Hide your head and hug the water

Lesson Four Practice Plan

The transition from drilling to swimming comes quickly and easily starting here. Lesson Four teaches you movements and coordination almost exactly the same as those you'll use in fluent swimming. You will probably not divide your time equally among all three drills in this lesson. As suggested above, spend lots of time on Zipper Skate to develop the great balance sense that will make you successful in the drills that follow. Spend enough time practicing Zipper Switch to master the switch timing. As your skills develop, spend more of your time with Triple Zipper because it teaches a range of valuable lessons and can do more than any other drill to make you a truly economical swimmer — one able to practically float through an Ironman swim leg without even breathing hard. See the next page for some suggested sequences.

100-yard repeats:

- 25 Zipper Skate on your right side, 25 Zipper Switch, 25 Zipper Skate left, 25 Zipper Switch
- 25 Under Switch, 25 Triple Under, 25 Zipper Switch, 25 Triple Zipper

150-yard repeats:

- 50 yards each (25 right, 25 left) of Drills 3, 4, and 9.
- 50 Zipper Skate (25 right, 25 left), 50 Zipper Switch, 50 Multi Zipper
- 25 Zipper Skate right, 25 Zipper Switch, 25 Triple Zipper + 25 Zipper Skate left, 25 Zipper Switch, 25 Triple Zipper

Extra Practice: More Zipper Switches

You can develop a tremendous amount of ease and flow with long, concentrated sessions of nothing but patient repetition of Triple Zipper (Drill #13). Limit yourself to 25-yard reps, resting between each rep for 3 to 5 yoga breaths. Give your attention to a single focal point on each repetition. Early stage practice should be mainly "block practice," i.e., allow 3 to 5 minutes of practice devoted to one focal point, followed by another 3 to 5 minutes concentrating on another focal point. After several weeks you can begin "random practice," that is, choosing a new focal point on each length and cycle through 100-yard sequences based on a series of four focal points. Here are suggestions:

1. **Hide your head.** Water should flow over the back of your head much of the time. Look straight down and watch yourself slide effortlessly past tiles on the pool bottom.

2. **"Hug" the surface..** Keep your head and elbows as close to the surface as possible, as if you were swimming under a very low ceiling.

3. **"Pierce" the water.** Slip through the smallest possible hole in space (above and below the surface.)

4. **Soften your arms and hands.** Sense the resistance of the water to your hand, but try to recover without creating turbulence or waves.

5. Feel the complete support of the water and use that support to bring your hand forward as slowly as you can.

6. Drill without making a sound.

7. And finally, once you have achieved true relaxation and ease, if you feel no need to breathe, **do more switches** — as many as 5 or 6 — before returning to Sweet Spot. Some swimmers find they can do effortless, unhurried Triple Zipper for a full 25 yards because they are so economical they use little oxygen to do a full pool length.

Lesson Five: Meet Your New Stroke

Lesson Four taught so many valuable skills and insights that Lesson Five will probably be the easiest of any lesson thus far. Lesson Five, though simple to master, will teach you precisely how your stroke will feel for the rest of your life. For some athletes Drills 12 & 13 **are** their form of "swimming," at least for a while. The great value of Lesson Five, particularly Drills 12 & 13 is that it gives almost anyone, even someone in the very early learning stages, an easy way to practice Fishlike Swimming.

Pre-practice Rehearsal: "Archer Timing"

For some swimmers, figuring out the right timing for Front-Quadrant Swimming (FQS) can be difficult. The trick is to determine where the recovering hand should be as the extended hand starts stroking and where the recovering hand should enter the water. This rehearsal smoothes the learning curve by letting you feel the right amount of overlap as one hand enters and the other makes its "catch."

Start by extending your left arm, while holding your right arm overhead, with your elbow above your right ear and pointing at the ceiling. Your right hand hangs at the edge of your goggles. (See photo.) Extend your right hand toward your left wrist, then draw it back toward your cheek and ear, just as an archer draws her bowstring. Memorize this position, then switch arms. Repeat several times, pausing to mark the position of your hands, arms, and raised elbow at the moment of the switch.

Drill #13: Over Switches

Why we do it: You've reached the final step in the drill-to-swimming process and we close our learning loop with a drill that teaches you how your new "Fishlike" stroke will feel. In fact, you'll be swimming with your new stroke between pauses in your Sweet Spot. This drill reinforces the timing you began imprinting with Under and Zipper Switch. That timing helps you swim *taller*. It also allows you to practice a deft, knifelike entry… Both of these skills help connect your arm to effortless power from core-body rotation.

Follow this sequence:

1. This drill is a natural extension of the corresponding drill in the Zipper drill series. Start with at least one full length of Triple Zipper. Make sure you're recovering with a compact, relaxed — almost lazy — recovery. On the second length (or later), begin with one cycle of Triple Zipper. Then, on the second cycle, raise your recovery hand so it barely clears the water and immediately re-enters. Do three or more "switches" on each cycle before going to Sweet Spot.

2. Practice with the following focal points:

• Keep your head hidden and stable. Keep watching the tiles on the pool bottom during the switches. Water should flow over the back of your head much of the time.

• Be "patient" on your switches: Wait for the recovering arm to reach your ear before you start to "pull" with your extended hand. Make the switch when you reach the "archer position" you memorized in the previous drill.

• Put your hand into the water right next to your goggles. Cut a hole with your fingers and slip your arm cleanly through that hole.

• Gradually shift focus from the timing of your switches to your *core-body-rolling rhythm*.

• Once you feel body rhythm, adjust body roll to allow for fluid, rhythmic, and seamless movement with no hesitation or interruptions.

3. If you feel good and don't particularly need to breathe, add switches. Most of our students can do four to six switches without feeling any distress. The key is to sustain a relaxed, effortless, switching-and-rolling rhythm. You may find yourself able to complete a full 25 yards without pausing in Sweet Spot.

Lesson Five Practice Plan

Except for the pauses in Sweet Spot, what you'll be practicing here in your multiple switches *is* swimming. You can use this practice to minimize the pressures or situations that might cause you to revert to your old "human-swimming" habits and to replace them with fluent movement. Particularly in early stages, it will be helpful to "tune up" for your Lesson Five practice with Lesson Four drills. And when you do concentrate on Lesson Five drills, use Over Switch mainly to refine timing and coordination. The more you develop as a swimmer, the more you should favor multiple (three or more) switch versions of the drills as they do more to imprint rhythmic movement.

Here are some suggested 150-yard sequences (continue to rest for 2 to 3 yoga breaths each 25):

- 25 Zipper Skate on your right side, 25 Zipper Switch, 25 Over Switch, 25 Zipper Skate left, 25 Zipper Switch, 25 Over Switch
- 25 Zipper Skate right, 25 Triple Zipper right, 25 Triple Over, 25 Zipper Skate left, 25 Triple Zipper, 25 Triple Over
- 50 Zipper Skate (25 right, 25 left), 25 Zipper Switch, 25 Triple Zipper, 25 Over Switch, 25 Triple Over

Find Your Bliss with Triple Over Switch

Concentrated practice of Triple Over can put you into a flow state. Do 25-yard reps (resting for 2 to 4 yoga breaths) for 7 to 15 minutes. Do block practice (attention to a single focal point for 3 to 5 minutes) in the beginning. Later shift to more random practice (cycle through a new focal point on each length in rounds of 3 to 4 x 25). Do 4 to 6 switches before pausing in Sweet Spot if you can. Relax in Sweet Spot for 3 yoga breaths. Here is a menu of focal points:

1. **Look down** so water flows over the back of your head.
2. **Lean in (swim downhill)** so your hips and legs feel light.
3. **"Hug" the surface.** Take your hand out of the water for the briefest possible period; put it back in right beside your goggles.

4. **"Pierce" the water.** Slip through the smallest possible space above and below the surface.

5. **Soften your recovery** and bring your hand forward as slowly as you can.

6. **Cut a hole with your knuckles (if wearing fistgloves®)** or fingertips and slip your entire arm through cleanly and steeply until it's below your head.

7. **Lengthen your vessel.** Feel your hand just float forward with no hurry.

8. **Time your switches consistently.**

9. **Move as silently as you can.**

Lesson Six: Making the Transition from Drilling to Swimming

Your swimming movements are all in place now. All that remains is to take out the Sweet Spot pauses and replace them with rhythmic breathing. Your goal here is to make breathing a seamless part of your body-rolling rhythm. (A secondary goal can be to breathe smoothly on either side.) Let's review what has prepared you to do this.

1. You learned to breathe by rolling your body to the air (rather than turning your head) in all three variations of Skating. Use Skating, Under Skate and Zipper Skate to reinforce that habit.

2. You learned to keep your head connected and aligned as you rolled to the air in Under Switch, Zipper Switch and Over Switch. Use those drills to reinforce this habit.

3. You developed your sense of core-body-rolling rhythms in Triple Zipper and Triple Over. Use those drills to reinforce your rhythm awareness.

4. You've worked on balance in all 13 drills. Improved balance will allow you to breathe without driving your lead arm toward the bottom. Focus on balance to "stay tall" as you breathe. Extensive use of fistgloves® in your practice — both drilling and swimming — can be particularly helpful in developing the "weightless arm."

We'll use Triple Over Switch as the basis for the transition to swimming. Do this with a series of 25-yard repeats. Rest as much as needed (no fewer than 5 yoga breaths) between reps to start each completely fresh. Start each rep with a normal (but water-piercing) pushoff and begin stroking with at least four switches before your first breath. This should not be a breath-holding effort, but a measure of how effortless you are. You should feel so relaxed that you can continue rhythmic weight shifts for quite a while before needing to breathe. The purpose of beginning the pool length with multiple uninterrupted switches is to establish your rhythm with core-body rotation and not with your arms. Once you feel an effortless, relaxed rhythm, you are ready to fit a breath into that rhythm with no interruption. Here's how.

1. Take your breath simply by *rolling right to where the air is* and immediately back in the other direction.

2. Try to do that with no interruption of the rolling rhythm you established on your switches before the breath.

3. If that breath goes smoothly, do another the same way, several strokes later. If you sense a slight interruption in your rhythm, try to smooth it out on the next stroke cycle.

4. If you lose control, *go back to Sweet Spot* on the next breath and think about how to improve your breathing technique on the next 25.

Be patient. Some athletes will fit breathing in seamlessly right away. Others, particularly those who have the most delicate sense of balance, may need to spend weeks learning to fit in a rhythmic breath without breaking down the control and coordination they have worked so diligently in drills to develop. Here are some tips that may help.

1.   A weightless arm is important. During multi-switch drills focus on having your arm float forward after entering next to your goggles. When you take your first breath, put particular focus on keeping that weightless-arm sensation. Your hand should keep inching forward while you breathe. *Fistgloves® will help!*

2.   Keep the timing of every switch exactly the same. Maintain that timing as you fit in your first breath.

3.   Roll as far as necessary. Old habits may be causing you to lift or turn your head. Keep everything connected and aligned as you roll your head, neck, and torso as one unit to air. *Roll all the way to the air.* If you're having difficulty getting air easily, roll *farther.*

4.   Slow down. Anytime you feel a loss of control, slow everything down. Be quieter and more gentle. Don't let yourself feel hurried. And finally, did I mention that *fistgloves® will help?*

Terry:

I wanted to touch base and let you know the results of the weekend workshop in Atlanta. I am amazed at what it has done for me and for my relationship with the water. I no longer dread getting in for endless laps, mainly because mindless swimming is no longer the focus. What I did not expect was how the experience would affect all my other training. I have been practicing my stroke drills diligently and am so thrilled with the way it brings pleasure and clear purpose to my training that I've begun to apply your mindfulness principle to my running and biking. Each time I go out to run or bike I focus on and practice one aspect of my technique for that workout. It really made me think about all the other training I've done in years past: endless miles or laps without focus and no purpose except conditioning for race day. I'm constantly learning more ways to apply focus every time I go out and it makes every training session interesting and rewarding in itself. My whole attitude has changed now and I'm so excited. Thank you so much.

Sincerely,

Michelle Judson

The lesson: The Total Immersion approach is not just a set of stroke drills; it's a holistic discipline for practicing flow-state training that can benefit all your physical activities. Learn the habit of focus in your practice of swimming, then apply it to every form of training you do.

Part 4

Smart Swimming for the Rest of Your Life

The first three sections of this book explained why swimming well is universally frustrating, but utterly essential, for triathletes. They also showed how easy it can be to become Fishlike, and took your stroke to school. Part 4 provides a plan for becoming your own best coach. If you train as suggested, I can promise all of the following:

1. You will see steady improvement in your efficiency and fluency...even if you continue swimming for another 30 years.

2. You will develop exactly the right kind of "swimming fitness" for triathlon success. Not the kind competitive swimmers need. The kind you need.

3. Swimming will become an increasingly satisfying way to exercise, very likely to the point where it becomes your favorite way to stay in shape, providing more physical and mental benefits with each passing year.

So let's dive right into your plan for using every minute of pool time effectively for continual improvement today and for as long as you swim.

Chapter 11

First Step: Use Your Existing Fitness More Effectively

It didn't take long after I swam my first race in 1966, for me to learn my place: I'm a pretty average athlete. Through high school, college, and Masters swimming I've recognized that other swimmers were born with a gift to swim faster than me: They could just dive in the pool and go fast while I always had to work long and hard to come even close to them. For a time, I believed that if I was willing to outwork them, I could close the gap. And, through sheer effort, I did narrow it, but I never became the equal of the really good athletes. So I gradually accepted my status — always a bit behind the best swimmers, but proud of having worked hard to get close.

But as I moved through my 40s and, now, past 50, I have renewed hope: I look more closely at those who are faster than me and — particularly in longer events — can see many opportunities to gain on them by working tirelessly to eliminate inefficiency. They may still have physical advantages but, as we age, physical capabilities diminish, while skill and efficiency may continue to increase. If I use my energy better as we all gradually lose the capacity to generate it I expect to become steadily more competitive. That prospect keeps my interest high.

As a triathlete, you probably have similar goals of improving your standing. Thus you probably do as I do — gauge your competitors and ask how you can improve your performance relative to theirs. In two of your sports, it will mainly be pure hard work that makes the difference. But in swimming, I guarantee it will be your *cleverness* in training that moves you ahead. Our training plan will show you how to make the absolute best use of every lap and hour of training, at whatever stage you may be in your development as a swimmer.

Training Happens

In developing a training plan for triathletes, I can't ignore the importance of fitness and conditioning. As an endurance athlete, I've come to view every physical thing I do as "training" and am always alert for opportunities to squeeze a bit more athletic value from it, whether it's swimming, biking, hiking with my family...even yard work.

This is also true of Total Immersion swim training. Conventional swim training focuses on building an aerobic base, raising the anaerobic threshold, developing lactate tolerance...through work, work, and more work. TI training puts your primary focus on learning to move efficiently and then expanding the range of distances and speeds at which you can do that. It shifts the focus from how much and how hard to *how right*. And the physiological stuff? Well, we define conditioning as "something that happens to you while you practice efficient swimming movements." And be assured that essential conditioning *does* happen, even while doing the gentlest of drills. For each type of TI training, I'll explain how it helps improve your fitness and why that form of training is important.

Functional, Not Generic, Training

Because endurance is the primary goal of triathlon training, we all know what it is — the capacity to do work without fatigue. The process of building endurance is like a chemistry experiment using your own body. You train your body to do a better job of storing food energy, converting it into muscle fuel, transporting it to your muscles (along with the oxygen needed to metabolize it) and remove waste products so your muscles can keep working at a high level. You improve those functions by...work.

When you do more work than your body is accustomed to — longer duration or higher intensity — your muscles and circulatory system develop the ability to circulate more blood with every heartbeat, to pack more beats into each minute, and to transport more oxygen and fuel in each blood cell. Because it seems so straightforward, we see the equation as pretty simple: More miles done harder and with less rest, produce all those desired adaptations.

And they do…when we're running or cycling. But the problem we face in swimming is that the "fuel tank" we're working so diligently to fill has a catastrophic leak. It's like this: As a runner you may be about 90 percent mechanically efficient. The fuel in your tank goes 90 percent into moving you down the road; 10 percent is lost to air resistance, road friction, and heat (sweat). But as a relatively new swimmer, you're more likely to be about *three percent* mechanically efficient; even Ian Thorpe is only 10 percent efficient — but he takes about 7 strokes for 25 yards while you may take three times that number. In that case, three calories of every 100 go directly into propulsion, while 97 are spent making waves and turbulence.

The reason for the huge disparity between swimming and running efficiency is the difference between propelling by pushing off solid ground and moving against air resistance, compared to propelling by pushing on water with your hand and moving through a medium that's 800 times thicker than air. And then there's the matter of mechanics. You learned to run reasonably well from a very young age; as a serious athlete, by concentrating on simple aspects of carriage and stride, you can approach the mechanical efficiency of elite runners. On your bike, your feet are strapped to the pedals, which can move in only one direction. If you learn a decent aero position, once again the efficiency puzzle is highly amenable to solution.

But in swimming, the range of possible movement choices is *enormous* and the room for error is vast. Only a tiny fraction of those choices are correct, and, because you're traveling through a fluid, the penalty for making the wrong choice is *huge*. Conventional swim training, with its focus on more and harder, is virtually guaranteed to force you into the wrong movement choices. Thus, the smart swimmer will adopt a more accurate definition for *swimming endurance*.

Instead of the capacity to push yourself through lap after lap without pause, your new definition is this: **Swimming endurance is the ability to repeat effective swimming movements (Stroke Length, economy, and fluency) for any duration, speed, and stroke rate that you choose.** It takes a specific kind of endurance to stay efficient and fluent for 20 to 60 seconds at a Stroke Rate of 100 strokes/minute and a very different sort to maintain good SL for 20 minutes to 2 hours at a SR of 50 to 60 strokes/minute.

Adopting this definition should motivate you toward the following training progression:

1. Eradicate your struggling skills and replace them with fluent movement skills.

2. Patiently turn those Fishlike movements into indelible habits.

3. Train yourself to systematically expand the range of distances, speeds, stroke rates and heart rates at which you can swim fluently.

As you spend hours doing this, *conditioning happens* — the right kind of conditioning. Neuromuscular training that ensures your muscles develop the right habits, and physiological training that ensures the *muscles that produce efficient movement* receive the benefit of the adaptations your training produces (rather than the ragged-movement muscles that are conditioned when you train by simple more-and-harder).

The Total Immersion training categories that correspond to the three goals stated above are 1) Learning, 2) Practice, and 3) Effective Swimming. Let's move straight to your plan for an effective Learning Stage.

Chapter 12

Learning to Move Efficiently

Y ou've undoubtedly succumbed to the temptation to get in the pool and start churning out laps; after all it's what *everyone* does. But until you learn balance — or *unlearn* your struggling skills — almost any whole-stroke swimming is likely to reinforce bad habits and delay progress toward fluency and efficiency. So your first step is to replace whole-stroke laps with *whatever allows you to practice fluent movement* and to avoid practicing struggle. For most of you, that means drills.

Your primary goal during the Learning Stage is to learn to do your drills impeccably. Part 3 provided exhaustive guidance on how to learn and practice drills. This chapter organizes that information into a training-and-development program. First a couple of rules for success in the Learning Stage:

1. When practicing drills, 100% right is 100% right; 95% right is *100% wrong*. As you progress through the six lessons — and particularly during the first two — you'll experience moments where you feel uncomfortable or lack coordination. Often it takes only a tiny adjustment, say in your body or head position, to make you feel *dramatically* better. Anytime you feel even a little bit uncomfortable, your natural reaction will be for some kind of compensation — craning your neck, using an arm as an "outrigger" for support, kicking too hard. The problem with these seemingly innocent reactions is that they imprint energy-wasting movements on your nervous system. So your constant goal is effortlessness and flow.

2. 100% right takes time and attention. Patience in mastering subtle movement skills may be natural to martial artists and dancers, but is an odd notion to most endurance athletes. I only came to appreciate its value after beginning yoga practice (see page 127). So here is your one goal for the next 10 to 20 hours of pool time: Simply learn to make mindful, examined movement a habit. Don't count laps or watch the pace clock; focus purely on reducing effort and increasing flow.

3. 95% of the 100% right will be determined by how well you master balance drills. Prioritize Lessons One and Two until balance becomes nearly effortless.

Organizing Your Practice

Successful drilling is your sole goal. Do whatever it takes to practice controlled, fluent movement and avoid struggle. *Everything else is secondary.* These practice-design tips will help.

Short repeats. At TI workshops, we teach Lessons I and II crosspool, not lengthwise. Because you move more slowly in static balance drills, even a trip of 10 to 12 yards can take time and be fatiguing, especially if you have a weak kick. Experience tells us that longer repeats mean 10 yards of reasonably good form followed by 15 yards of progressive struggle. We don't want that part imprinted on the nervous system so we stop at 10 yards. Your Learning Stage repeats should mainly be 25s and 50s. Your rule for how far is: Every lap should feel as good or better than the first. If it doesn't, **stop and rest** — even mid-lap.

Short sets. Once you've gotten past learning the drills and have begun assembling a number of 25s or 50s into sets, limit yourself mainly to sets that last about 10 minutes. Beyond that, mental acuity is usually not as good, so take a break or work on something that requires a bit less concentration or simply shift to another drill or focal point to renew your attention.

Super-slow movement. Crawl before walking and walk before running. Do all swimming movements well *slowly* before trying to do them faster. Go no faster at any time than your ability to maintain complete control of the movement. If you find yourself, because of better balance or sleeker body positions, seeming to move a little faster, you should mainly be marveling at how little effort it takes to do so.

Do one thing well. Avoid paralysis by analysis. Use the focal points listed for each drill in Lessons One to Six. Give all of your attention to just one point on each pool length. On the next length, either focus on the same point again, or shift to a new one, but think about doing just one thing well and trust your body to use the imprinting you've done at other times of other focal points. Over time, they will all harmonize and integrate smoothly.

Super Silent. Quieter drilling is *always* better. Once you've mastered the mechanics of a drill, one of the simplest things you can do to improve your drill quality is to do it more quietly.

Give yourself enough rest. When you take a break at the wall, you're not on a "schedule" to push off again. Listen to your body. It has a pretty good sense of the difficulty of what you're asking it to do. Just ask: "Am I ready to do that a little better than last time?" Begin again when you feel prepared to do the drill well. And use "yoga breaths" or bobs to set your intervals.

Training Happens

You can make training as complicated or as simple as you like. I have all the "authoritative" swimming tomes that describe aerobic training effects in terms like "concentrates muscle enzymes such as succinate dehydrogenase," but I can't recall an instance when one of my swimmers approached a race more confidently because their enzymes were concentrated. On the other hand, when they master a balance drill and can *feel* that their hips and legs are lighter than ever before, they *know* something has happened that will help them swim faster.

But be assured that, as you practice things that make you feel lighter in the water, training *does* happen. Your physiology receives essential benefits in the Learning Stage and in every form of Total Immersion training, both drills and whole-stroke swimming. I prefer to use terms such as "super-slow, cruise, brisk, and race-effort" to describe the physiological goal of a set because they are more easily grasped than a term like "anaerobic threshold." But aerobic capacity *will* be increased in specific ways by each efficiency-building exercise I prescribe. The main difference between TI training and conventional training is that we make the goal of building and imprinting efficiency the central focus, while physiologic gains happen in the background. Conventional training makes "concentration of enzymes" the central goal while "technique practice" becomes an after-thought — something you do for 10 minutes at the end of your workout.

Because you can add speed by subtracting drag or energy cost far more quickly than you can do it by adding fitness or strength, it makes far more sense to put efficiency-training at the heart of what you do in the pool while the physiology becomes incidental.

The TI/RPE Scale

Swedish physiologist Dr. Gunnar Borg developed a scale of training intensities to help cardiac-rehab patients monitor the intensity of their exercise. This scale, known as Rate of Perceived Exertion (RPE), has proven effective for athletes as well. Though various versions of his scale have 10 to 20 levels, I find that for most athletes, six divisions allow you to cut it as finely as you need. Here is the Total Immersion RPE Scale, which assigns a number between one and six to your perception of how hard you are working, as well as what your TI-training emphasis will be:

1. Literally effortless. Super slow. Very examined. Best for learning new skills. Approximately 50% of Maximum Heart Rate.

2. Warmup/warmdown speed. Easy and slow. Good for recovery/restoration...and for imprinting good stroke habits. 60% of MHR.

3. Cruise speed. A level of effort you could maintain for a set of 20 to 30 minutes in training or perhaps up to 2.4 miles in an Ironman race if your stroke efficiency is well developed. If you were running, this would be called "conversational pace" ...though your sentences might be brief. Only a moderate challenge to maintain SL and fluency. A good level for swim-leg race rehearsal. 70% of MHR.

4. Brisk. Moderately hard. You could maintain this effort level for repeats of 100 to 200 yards in training, for a sprint distance swim leg, or for occasional bursts — say, to pass someone — in a 1-kilometer or longer swim leg. But you need to concentrate to avoid struggle. A more important training pace for swim-only races than for tri-swim races. 80% of MHR.

5. Fast. Working hard enough to become breathless and to experience a degree of discomfort. Requires intense concentration to maintain good form. An advanced swimmer might work this hard while swimming 25s or 50s or well-rested 100s in training, but few triathletes would ever swim this hard in a race. On the other hand, if you do Masters swimming (200 to 500 yards), you could find yourself racing at this level. 90% of MHR.

6.   Absolute Maximum. Triathletes have no need to ever swim at this level, unless you plan to race short sprints (100 or shorter) in Masters swimming. 100% of MHR.

While in the Learning Stage, you'll do all of your training in Levels 1 and 2 of TI/RPE. Your efforts will be more mental than physical as your drill practice will benefit most from keen concentration and complete comfort. You are trying to become effortless in your movements.

The purely physiological benefits in this stage will be twofold:

1.   Aerobic Base Building. If you're a budding triathlete, you probably aim to train five to 10 hours a week. If you're a serious one, you probably train 10 to 20 hours a week. Simply being able to sustain a weekly volume like that takes a foundation of aerobic fitness. That kind of foundation is developed through exercise that's *extensive*, not intensive — gentle enough to be sustained, without fatigue, for an hour or more. If you are a beginning athlete, that means really, *really* easy. If you are an experienced athlete, but an *inexperienced* swimmer, that means *swimming* really, really easily. Even if you are an experienced swimmer, but inexperienced in these new techniques, the same thing applies as you learn them. If you're not making yourself tired, you can stay in the pool for longer periods, giving yourself more time to imprint good skills. The extensive, low-effort exercise prescribed in the Learning Stage helps develop the cardiovascular foundation for efforts of greater duration — the 10-hour training week, the 2- to 3-hour race — and eventually for efforts of higher intensity.

2.   Restoration. Because you're a triathlete, you'll train in at least three sports and possibly weightlifting or other cross-training. At times, you'll be over-trained — tired, sore, or heavy-legged. Only one form of training has the potential for truly assisting in your recovery. That's swimming, because of the absence of gravity, the massaging effect of moving gently in water, and because maintaining blood flow through sore, tired limbs helps to flush them out. Thus, recovery often happens more quickly and completely with gentle swimming than with simple inactivity. Learning Stage practice thus affords three benefits at the same time: recovery for sore or tired muscles, maintenance of the aerobic base, and skill improvement. That's a lot of value to pack into an hour.

Advancing to Practice

There's no hard and fast rule for earning promotion from Learning to Practice Stage nor any firewall between one stage and another. Common sense is the only rule. Focus on activities you do well and easily. Minimize or avoid those you find difficult until you learn to do them with more ease. You may advance from Learning to Practice fairly quickly in basic skills, such as balance, while finding yourself in Learning mode two or three years down the road for advanced skills such as maintaining impeccable balance while breathing or staying fluent while swimming briskly. Most likely you'll be doing 85% Learning, 10% Practice, and 5% Effective Swimming over the first few months on the TI program. Six months later, that mix may shift to 60% Learning, 25% Practice and 15% Effective Swimming. My own program, after many years of teaching and practice, is about 5% Learning (there will always be *some* aspect of technique that requires intense concentration), 45% Practice, and 50% Effective Swimming.

You can do whole-stroke swimming at the Practice Stage, but use the same guidelines as for drills: short repeats (25 to 50 yards), slow speeds, and focus purely on ease and control. Think about doing just one thing really well when you swim. Refer to the menu of Sensory Skill Practice focal points in the next chapter for suggestions.

Effort and Surrender

It was the poster that got my attention. The one that appeared in New Paltz store windows announcing a new yoga center. It pictured an 85-year old woman in the Warrior position, showing more grace, strength, and suppleness than all but the most athletic teenager. It said that she had not begun practicing yoga until age 65. I thought of myself as rather athletic for age 48, but there was no way I could have done that position that impressively. In fact, for a month or two I had been feeling almost crippled by a recurring back problem. Swimming is supposed to be good for your back but it was doing nothing for mine.

So I purchased a membership that allowed me three months of unlimited classes and began attending classes almost daily. Within a month my back problem — which, for five years had resisted every high-tech solution short of surgery — was history. Within three months I felt taller and straighter than I had in 25 years. And, when I recently turned 50, I was more supple than at any time I can recall.

Two years of yoga practice have also yielded several dividends I never expected. Though I signed on for the physical benefits, yoga practice has taught me countless lessons about how to teach and practice swimming skills more effectively. The penetrating attention that one learns in practicing the *asanas* is an incredibly valuable habit for practicing stroke drills. As I gradually realized, the point of doing asanas is not to touch your toes more easily, but to learn concentration, self-awareness, self discipline and how to "balance effort and surrender." Though I realize I have only scratched the surface, I still have learned more than I expected about how to use my body more intelligently.

I also continue to discover opportunity for refining movements that I had thought were pretty good already. Though I've done the triangle pose nearly a thousand times, I still manage to improve a bit each time I twist into it. Perhaps pressing the outer heel of my back foot into the floor a bit more firmly…or holding my upstretched arm just a bit straighter above my nose…or rotating back my upper shoulder ever so slightly. And — because my body resists each of those fine adjustments — to "breathe away" tension and allow straining muscles to work with, not against, one another. Gradually, I learn to maintain the pose in a calm — almost detached — way, without fatigue, for as long as I wish.

Whatever you may do that helps you understand your body better, to be more aware of positioning and alignment, to reduce the energy cost of movements and positions, will serve you well no matter how advanced your swimming may become. Am I saying you need to begin attending yoga classes? Well, it wouldn't hurt if you did — I've found yoga to be far superior to any "swimming stretches" for developing the kind of strength and range of motion that I feel when swimming fluently. But if your schedule is already too packed for one more activity, you *can* adopt a "yoga mentality" in your drill practice. By now you may already be yoga-breathing. But you can achieve more mastery in your drill practice by adopting certain attitudes about your drill practice.

Zen Drilling

The Iyengar style of yoga I've been studying is noted for the slow, precise, and concentrated way in which it is practiced. This experience has given me a greater understanding and appreciation for the following qualities:

Awareness. Moving slowly and with great control and concentration allows me to more fully inventory how my body reacts, particularly when I attempt something unfamiliar. In order to swim with the sort of flow and economy that I describe as "Fishlike," swimmers must master a whole range of new skills, none of which is intuitive or instinctive. In order to learn them smoothly, you must first develop self-awareness as a habit, which will in turn reveal the importance of:

Stillness. In yoga, you prepare yourself to do the new or difficult by first becoming still, composed and balanced, then retaining those qualities as you explore the new or difficult. I have learned to emphasize that quality in the execution of skill drills in my teaching. Learn stillness in Lessons One and Two and cultivate it in Sweet Spot in the advanced drills.

Economy. Doing something new or difficult usually involves a certain degree of strain. When moving to a more advanced yoga position, I've noticed that, at first, I tend to over-react to its difficulty. I "try" too hard. But by backing off a bit and approaching it more gently, I can pare down my reaction. With more practice I can gradually execute the new skill with greater economy. When prescribing a series of repeats of a new drill to triathletes in a workshop, I strongly emphasize the importance of doing "less" on each successive repetition — to execute it with increasing economy of motion.

Relaxed precision: We are more powerful when relaxed. We are less effective when tense. Relaxed precision and effortless ease are the key to transforming *forcing* into *flowing*. At the very highest level of mastery are those swimmers who can maintain relaxed precision in the heat of a race — particularly a sprint race. In yoga, when trying to perfect a difficult (and possibly uncomfortable) pose, we work on "balancing effort and surrender." Do the same when you find a drill difficult. When doing whole-stroke swimming, avoid "struggling" to swim fast.

Drill like an artist, not an athlete. Seek easier and less, rather than harder and more. In a fluid medium, what could be more important than flow?

Chapter 13

Practice: Making Fluent Movement a Habit

P
eople usually have no idea what they look like while swimming. They may vaguely sense that their stroke is choppy or uncoordinated, but they don't *really* know until they see themselves on video. Which is why the underwater video we shoot at TI workshops and view in slow motion is such an eye-opener.

We videotape each class on Saturday morning, before we begin teaching. After lunch, we show it to a rapt audience, who understand immediately why their swimming has been so frustrating or exhausting. Upon viewing their awkward and angular positions, our students leave the state of *unconscious incompetence* (being unaware or unclear what they're doing wrong) and achieve *conscious incompetence*. They know exactly what they have to fix and why. They may not yet know how to fix it, but the video is a powerful motivator for change.

The following afternoon, after six to seven hours of teaching, we videotape again. The image moving far more smoothly across the TV monitor offers vivid confirmation of how much they have improved. *But* they also recognize that the painstaking concentration that went into swimming 25 yards with a longer and more coordinated stroke is just a starting point, called *conscious competence*. They've learned to do some things right, but if asked to swim just a little farther — say, 100 yards — or a bit faster, they'd have a hard time maintaining their hard-won skills.

Their longer-term goal is to reach the stage of *unconscious competence* where they can swim efficiently and fluently for nearly any distance and at moderately fast speeds.

The difference isn't simply in distance or speed; it's also in your ability to move with effortless grace. Consider the simple act of brushing your teeth. Having done this perhaps 30,000 times over the years, your "brushing practice" has produced "brushing skill" that lets you do it expertly without even thinking. But what if you brushed with your other hand? It would take a lot more conscious control simply to avoid injury. That's the difference between conscious competence and unconscious competence. Only when a skill becomes autonomic can it acquire effortless flow.

The only way to take a skill from conscious to unconscious competence is by performing thousands of *correct* repetitions. Anything else just confuses your nervous system. So our goal as we begin Practice Stage activities is to practice your developing skills often enough to allow them to become automatic — and to avoid doing things that cause you to revert to "struggling skills."

An important part of this process, after you develop balance and begin to erase your struggling habits in the Learning Stage, is to gradually "take off the training wheels" by replacing drilling with whole-stroke swimming. You can avoid being pulled back toward "human swimming" and imprint only *correct repetitions* in your "skill bank" by being scrupulous about swimming with as much fluency and ease as in your basic drills. Here's the progression:

1.   Mix some whole-stroke swimming into your drill sets

2.   Introduce simple, narrowly focused, swimming-only sets, designed to make it easy to begin swimming with good SL, control, and coordination.

3.   Practice enough *correct* reps to make fluency and SL a habit and by making choices to avoid struggle.

1. From Drills to Swimming

Your drill practice has begun to build good movement habits, good practice habits and a keen awareness of the difference between flow and struggle. That awareness is at the heart of how to use drills to become a better swimmer. Drills transform largely by providing powerful insights into how fluent swimming *feels*, as if you were able to do a "virtual lap" inside the skin of a skilled swimmer. In drill-swim sets, simply ask yourself "What feels different and better about this drill, compared to how swimming usually feels?" Then maintain that feeling for as long as you can while swimming whole stroke. The moment you lose it, *stop swimming*.

How many laps of drill and how many of swim? Drill until it feels just right; at first that may take 100 yards (4 x 25) or more. Then continue swimming for as long as your stroke feels as good as the drill, which, initially, may be only 25 yards. So, your first drill-swim sets may be 3 or 4 lengths of drill to every length of swim. As you get better at both, it may take only 50 yards of drill to feel just right and you may be able to swim feeling *that good* for the same distance. Ultimately, you'll find that it takes only a brief reminder, perhaps 25 yards of drill, to nail that feeling and you can sustain it while swimming for 3 to 5 lengths.

Keep Your Focus

In Chapter 12, I suggested that you think about doing only one thing really well during the Learning Stage. That's still the rule here. If you alternate 25 yards of Skating with 25 of swimming, and are focused mainly on keeping your head hidden during the drill, then think only about your head position as you swim. Here are some other suggested combinations of drill and focal point for drill and swim:

Under Skate. Roll like a needle to breathe; roll all the way to the air.

Zipper Skate. "Lean on your lungs" with light hips and legs; being completely supported by the water.

Under-Switch. Roll freely as you swim.

Zipper Switch. "Pierce" the water; fit your body through the smallest hole as you swim.

Over Switch. Stay "connected" (close the gap between shoulder and head) as you swim; swim with your whole body.

Triple Under Switch. Extend a weightless arm on each stroke.

Triple Zipper Switch. Have a soft, gentle, compact recovery; your hand barely clears the water and re-enters immediately.

Triple Over Switch. Cut a hole with your fingertips and slip your arm cleanly through that hole as you swim.

You're certainly not limited to these. In Chapters 4 through 9 I gave many focal points for improving your stroke and, during the Lessons, I gave multiple focal points for every drill. Use any of them during drill-swim sets and eventually you'll develop some favorites.

When you first do Drill-Swim sets, start with Block practice — maintaining one focus or sensation for at least 5 to 10 minutes. Later, as the sensation becomes second nature, shift gradually to Random practice, sequencing different drills and different focal points every minute or two. If you feel confusion, make it less random, but random practice, by making your brain process new skill info more frequently, can help accelerate your progress toward unconscious competence.

Go Easy on Yourself

Follow the same practice techniques you adopted in the Learning stage. Go as slowly as necessary to move with flow and ease. Take enough rest to ensure that every repeat is as good as the first — or as good as the *best*. Ignore the pace clock and focus purely on how you feel. Use yoga breathing for your rest interval — and rest frequently; 50 to 100 yards is far enough to drill/swim without pause. Limit your sets to 10 to 15 minutes. In fact, don't begin a set with the intent to do a particular number of reps or yards. Instead, check the minute hand on the pace clock and plan to simply practice a particular skill with blissful ease and flow until a set amount of time has elapsed. When the minute hand has advanced 10 or 15 minutes, the set is complete and you have just had an incredibly valuable period of imprinting.

2. Super-Slow Swimming (SSS)

Over the years I have steadily increased my Stroke Length and steadily reduced the number of strokes it takes me to swim 25 or 100 or 1000 yards. My lowest count for swimming 100 yards was about 60 strokes in 1970 as a college swimmer. By the early 90s my stroke count for a leisurely 100 was down to 50, but the thought of doing it in 45 or 46 strokes was unimaginable. But in April 2001, I swam 100 yards in 39 effortless, fluid, and rhythmic strokes.

The key was Super-Slow Swimming: In order to travel 100 yards in 39 strokes, I swam as slowly as I could…without losing my balance or rhythm or turning it into a drill. SSS offers two primary benefits: It allows maximum concentration and "purposeful exaggeration." To experience the concentration possible, try doing a single pushup…as…slowly…as…possible. Doing a pushup super-slowly will incredibly heighten your awareness of all the muscular interaction required for a pushup. You'll not only feel every chest, shoulder, arm, and back muscle that provides leverage but also realize how much abdominal muscle you use to stabilize your torso as you lower and lift it. SSS gives you greater awareness of all the forces that resist you and the counter-forces you use to overcome that resistance. Such slow movement allows you to minimize and maximize those forces as never before.

The second benefit is the opportunity to bring "purposeful exaggeration" (see Chapter 10) to whole-stroke swimming. The Fishlike Swimming techniques that make you far more efficient and effective are almost completely counter-intuitive. We make them feel more natural, in part, by exaggerating them slightly in our practice. The leisurely tempo of SSS leaves a lot more "room" in each stroke cycle for that exaggeration.

I've been able to achieve super-low stroke counts while doing SSS because I had the time to keep extending my hand a bit longer…to rotate my body just a bit farther…to "skate" past another couple of lane markers during my recovery…and to achieve more front-quadrant overlap on my switches. Having practiced and imprinted all those efficiency builders to an extra degree while swimming super slowly gives me something to "trade" as I increase my Stroke Rate and swim faster. The result is that I retain more of a hydrodynamic advantage — which reduces my energy cost — at any higher speed than swimmers who do not practice SSS and purposeful exaggeration.

What's the benefit of the super-low stroke count I can achieve at slow speeds? When my lowest count for 100 yards was 50 strokes (about 13 strokes/length) my time for 100@50 was only about 1:24. Now that I can do 100@39, my time for 100@50 is about 1:14. When 100@50 was the best I could do, I could sustain that count of 13 spl for only a few lengths. Now I can maintain 13 spl for nearly any distance, which means my SL and economy for distance swimming have improved markedly.

One more thought on SSS: Those low counts must be effortless. If you make yourself tired and breathless at a low stroke count, you're simply practicing a less-frantic form of struggle. You must have impeccable balance to make SSS fully beneficial. You need to feel that it's the complete support of the water that gives you the freedom to float your hand forward a bit farther...to rotate your body a bit more...to "skate" past another few lane markers in each stroke cycle. Remember that your "best" SL is always one you can achieve with a minimum of effort.

3. Sensory Skill Practice (SSP)

In November of 2000, I raced 800 meters at a Masters meet. Employing my usual negative-split strategy, I began with a relaxed, controlled first 200, then picked up the pace and tempo in each successive 200, finishing strongly and passing several other swimmers over the last half of the race. Checking my splits and seeing that my final 200 was my fastest, I was congratulating myself on another race plan successfully executed. Until Lisa Bauman, the coach of Aquafit Masters on Long Island (and someone I coached 25 years earlier) came up and said, "Terry, do you know that you stopped rotating your hips on the last 200? You rolled to your left to breathe but never rolled to your right."

Oops. Well, I *had* felt far less smooth, but I thought it was just end-of-race fatigue. Pondering it, I realized that I had sacrificed rotation to increase Stroke Rate, which left me swimming mainly with my arms. The touchpad came just in time; I was toast at the end. Fortunately I knew how to fix it...permanently. For the next three months, I spent about 70 percent of my practice time focusing on just one thing: after each left side breath, I would drive my "high" (left) hip down, ensuring that I rotated completely to my right.

When I swam super slowly, I drove the hip down slowly. When I went a little faster, I drove the hip down more briskly. Most important, whenever I swam at near race pace — where things had broken down in the 800 — I focused relentlessly on creating that speed mostly by driving my left hip down faster and more forcefully. Two months later at my next meet, I had driven my high hip down tens of thousands of times. My narrow focus resulted in a strikingly improved race experience: fast closing splits that felt much stronger and smoother.

This is just one illustration of the value of what I call Sensory Skill Practice: a focus on doing *just one thing* well. I have already suggested it as a useful technique for drill practice and drill-swim sets. As you do more whole-stroke sets it's one of the easiest ways to simplify what may seem like a monumental task of coordinating all the fine skills of Fishlike Swimming. Here's a menu of sensory cues you can use in your whole-stroke practice:

Hide Your Head

Lead with the top of your head, not your forehead.

Feel water flowing over the back of your head much of the time.

See the bottom directly under you, and not much that's forward of you.

Swim Downhill

Lean on your chest until your hips and legs feel light.

Rhythmically press in one armpit, then the other.

Feel completely supported by the water.

Lengthen Your Body

Extend a weightless arm.

Be able to float your arm forward for a l-o-n-g time.

Reach for the far wall before stroking.

Put your arm into the water as if sliding it into a sleeve.

Keep extending your arm until you feel your shoulder touch your jaw or ear.

Practice Your Switches

Make a hole with your fingertips and slip your whole arm cleanly through that hole.

Feel "archer timing" in your stroke.

Clear the water by the slightest margin on recovery.

Have your hand out of the water for the shortest possible time on recovery.

Anchor Your Hands

Make your hands *stand still* as you begin each stroke.

Move your body past your hand, rather than pushing back.

Never move your hand *back* faster than your body is moving *forward*.

Swim faster with your *whole body* not your arms and legs.

Skate and Rotate

Feel yourself slide effortlessly past a few lane markers before stroking.

Breathe by rolling to where the air is.

Drive the high hip down on every stroke.

"Look" at each wall with your belly-button in each stroke.

Slippery Swimming

Pierce the water; slip through the smallest possible hole.

Maintain a low profile, as if swimming under a very low ceiling.

Silent Swimming

Drill or swim as quietly as possible.

When increasing your speed (descending sets or negative splits) try not to make more noise.

How SSPs Work

If you've swum with your head high forever (you know, *millions* of strokes), you have carved a deep groove in your nervous system for a high head position. You might be able to "hide" your head if you *really* think about it, but it will probably feel unnatural, and the moment you stop thinking about it — perhaps to think about extending a weightless arm — chances are your head will pop up again. But each lap you consciously focus on hiding your head faintly imprints a new groove in your nervous system. After five or ten minutes thinking only about that, it will feel a bit more natural and you improve the chances that you'll keep doing it when you're *not* thinking about it. Each time you devote another ten minutes to it, proper head position becomes a bit more permanent.

If you take all those focal points mentioned above and give time to each of them, the incredibly complex business of a really efficient stroke will gradually assemble itself in a pretty seamless way. With each passing hour, week, and month of purposeful practice, each piece will be polished on its own and fit a bit more naturally with all the other pieces, while you avoid ever becoming overwhelmed by the sheer complexity of it all.

How long will it take until your new stroke is perfect and permanent? The rest of your life! The polishing process should never end; you can continue improving endlessly. But my rule of thumb for getting a skill to the point where it's a "no-brainer" — to the point where you'll always do it even when you're not thinking about it — is 100,000 yards. That's not to say that you should think only about hiding your head for the next 4000 laps, but by the time you *have* devoted 4000 laps to that focus, it should be permanent.

How to Practice SSPs

As with drills and drill-swim sets, start using SSPs by choosing one focal point and sticking with it for 10 or more minutes of highly attentive practice, before shifting your focus to another one. As that way of swimming feels more natural, alternate it with other SSPs with gradually increasing frequency. Here's an example:

Block Practice

300 yards of Hiding Your Head + 300 yards of Weightless Arm + 300 yards of Archer Timing + 300 yards of Driving the High Hip Down.

Random Practice

3 rounds of: (100 yards of Hiding Your Head + 100 yards of Weightless Arm + 100 yards of Archer Timing + 100 yards of Driving the High Hip Down).

Very Random Practice

12 x 100 as: (25 Hiding Your Head + 25 Weightless Arm + 25 Archer Timing + 25 Driving the High Hip Down). Don't practice like this until each of those skills feels like a "no-brainer" on its own.

Open-Water Rehearsal

One of the best applications of SSPs is for purposeful open-water practice. One drawback of doing SSPs in a pool is this experience: You push off and begin working on making your hands *stand still*. After 10 or 12 strokes you start to become attuned to what your hands do in that fleeting moment just before stroking and *think* you can anchor them just a bit. Then the wall interrupts your concentration and you have to start all over again. Just as you begin to feel it, you lose the flow. So a 50-meter pool is far better than a 25-yard pool for this. Better yet would be a "pool" that's 400 meters or a mile long — i.e., a calm lake or reservoir or cove.

In open water, you can "groove" that sensation and then just keep going for a hundred or more strokes of profound imprinting. Even better, you can use SSP as rehearsal. Experiment with a number of focal points and see which make you feel the best. Then, on race day, you know exactly how to put yourself in a flow state. And if conditions change (more chop or higher swells, for instance), you can try out a variety of SSPs to see which work best in various conditions. Practicing SSPs for a set number of strokes in open water gives purpose and organization to formerly aimless open-water training and is the best possible rehearsal.

* * *

We've finished our lessons, progressed through the stage of making those formerly alien-feeling movements a bit more natural and begun to turn them into rock-solid habits. By now, you're probably itching to do a real workout. We have that for you, too, but with a critical TI tweak — time to move on to Effective Swimming.

Effective Swimming: The Smartest Way to Train

Alan, a budding triathlete of enormous promise, swims in the Masters group where I train. Just a few years removed from college track, boasting impressive 10K times, he quickly became a force on the bike. When I first time met him, eight months ago, I was amazed at how beautifully he swam. I was paddling a canoe, taking my turn as lifeguard for the open-water group we swim with in the summer, when I saw a tall, lanky figure gliding through the water with long, balanced, smooth strokes. I was impressed to discover that such a good runner with no real swimming background could swim so beautifully. But Alan instinctively knew the right way and thus had all the ingredients for real success in triathlon.

A few weeks ago, watching him again near the end of a Masters workout, I was surprised again...but this time less favorably. His fluent, effective stroke had become rushed and choppy — not auspicious for open-water success. How had Alan lost his form? Very simple: Replacing nearly languorous, untimed lake swims with *workouts* — repeats, tight intervals, chasing (or being chased by) lane-mates, urgings from the coach to go **hard** — had shifted Alan's focus from *just feeling good in the water* to *working hard in the water*. It appeared to me as if the main dividend of eight months of faithful workout attendance was lost efficiency.

Having come this far, don't let that happen to you. This chapter will give you a detailed plan for putting your energy into the most beneficial kind of training: workouts (I prefer to call them "practices") that not only increase your fitness, but also train you to maximize it with the kind of efficiency that makes elite swimmers so much better than the rest of us.

Traditional workouts are virtually always focused on racing the pace clock and/or other swimmers. As anyone who has done swimming workouts knows, the longer the set...the faster the pace...the tighter the interval...the harder it is to maintain your efficiency. The upshot is that even as you give your all to getting stronger and fitter, powerful "human swimming" instincts are limiting your potential because virtually everything that happens while *working out* pushes you to use more SR and less SL to make those intervals and descend those sets.

The key to training intelligently and effectively is never to lose sight of the importance of the equation **V = SL X SR.** The world's best swimmers are faster than you because they travel so much farther on every stroke cycle, not because they move their arms faster. From now on, if you aren't doing Learning or Practice sets, you should be doing Effective Swimming. The difference between Effective Swimming and conventional training is constant awareness of SL *and* awareness that any time you're *not* monitoring SL, it's very likely that habit and instinct will cause you to use too much SR.

Effective Swimming sets do two incredibly valuable things: (1) Encourage you to use more SL and (2) Alert you immediately when you don't — i.e., when you revert to the Human Swimming tendency to use too much SR. And all you have to do is begin counting your strokes. For the rest of your life, if you're not doing a drill, or focusing on an SSP, you should count your strokes.

Initially, counting strokes will take nearly all of your brainpower. That's why you'd find it difficult in the first couple of months to put sufficient focus on an SSP *and* count strokes. But, as you do it regularly, it will require less concentration. Before long, you'll be counting almost automatically. So automatically that you may find it hard *not* to count strokes — your hand goes in, your brain registers "One." So automatic that you'll be able to even do semi-advanced *math* in creative combinations of stroke count and time. So let's get started on constant SL awareness.

Finding Your SL

Let's cover some basics first. How to count? Some count *stroke cycles*, e.g., counting only right hand entries. I prefer counting each stroke for slightly finer accuracy, and I do so as each hand enters the water. In effect, I'm counting the stroke as I finish it.

Next, is there a particular stroke count you should aim for? Not at first. Just start counting and simply take note of what that tells you. If you swim a *consciously competent* 25 yards and take 16 strokes, you have the first bit of information that will gradually evolve into a keen awareness of the challenge of conserving efficiency as you swim farther or faster. If you swim 50 yards and take 16 strokes going and 19 coming, you've learned that it's difficult to maintain your initial stroke efficiency. You can then set a simple goal: To swim 50 yards in 16+18, doing a little better job of maintaining your efficiency as distance increases. If you swim 25 yards at a slightly brisker pace and see your stroke count rise from 16 to 18, you have another important piece of information...and you can set another goal: Find a way to add a bit of speed without giving up quite as much SL.

Doing the simplest stroke-counting sets as suggested below will help you establish a stroke-count *range* and learn the lowest stroke count you can swim at *any* speed with a minimum of effort and a maximum of flow and rhythm. In the beginning, for super-slow 25s, a rhythmic and smooth 14 strokes per length (spl) might be better than a lurching, heavy-kicking 12 spl, but in a few weeks you may learn to swim a rhythmic and smooth 12 spl. Over time, with more practice and increased efficiency, your stroke count range should both get lower and narrower. You may find your initial range, for instance, to be 14 to 24. In three months that may improve to 12 to 20 and in a year to 10 to 16. Once you know your range, plan to do 75% of your training in the lower half of your range.

How this benefits you can easily be understood with a weight-lifting analogy. Let's say your record for one bench press is 120 pounds. When working with 110 pounds, you might be able to lift it only three times. But as your maximum improves to 140 pounds, you'd probably be able to lift 110 pounds ten or more times. As your SL improves, you'll be able to do more at every count above your minimum. When your lowest spl is 14, you might be able to swim only two or three lengths at an average of 15 spl. And your pace for 50 yards at 15 spl might only be 50 seconds. But when your lowest spl drops to 12, you'll probably find you can swim as much as 500 or 1000 yards at 15 spl and that your pace for 50 yards might have improved to 45 seconds when you allow yourself the "luxury" of taking 15 strokes.

Start Counting

The following exercises are a good way to get started. They will allow you to begin developing some SL benchmarks, to learn how distance or speed or stroke tweaks may affect your SL, and to begin working on self-adjusting your SL. Use yoga breaths, rather than the pace clock, to set rest intervals. It's not necessary to do all six exercises in one session. Just do a couple, as a way of beginning to include some Effective Swimming with your drill and SSP practice. Some days you might do one of the exercises several times with a goal of improving on subsequent rounds. But don't do them to the point of fatigue or raggedness. Call it a day or return to easier drilling, rather than practice struggle. Experienced swimmers are welcome to double the repeat distances (50-100-150-200), but anyone can learn valuable lessons while doing the basic sets.

SL Exercise #1

Swim 25+50+75+100. Rest for 3 to 5 yoga breaths after each swim.

Take note of your stroke count on the 25, then *without trying to strictly limit* your count, just swim at a consistent pace or effort and see what happens to your spl average on the other swims. If you took 15 strokes for the 25, how far above 30-45-60 strokes are you on the 50-75-100? Again, just take note and file the information away for future reference.

SL Exercise #2

Swim 100+75+50+25. Rest for 3 to 5 breaths after each swim.

Start with an easy 100. Count your strokes and divide by four. This number becomes your "N" (benchmark spl count) for the rest of the set. E.g., If you took 72 strokes, your N is 18 spl (72 divided by four lengths). Again, simply note how far below 54-36-18 strokes you are for 75-50-25.

SL Exercise #3

Swim 25+50+75+100.

Repeat Exercise #1, but this time with a focus on any SSP — perhaps hiding your head, or slipping through a smaller hole, or swimming more quietly. Again, just take note of your stroke count; don't attempt to hit any particular count. This is purely an experiment to see if technique "tweaks" affect your SL. If so, this exercise demonstrates that you *can* affect — and ultimately *choose* your SL.

SL Exercise #4

Swim 2 rounds of: 25+50+75+100.

1st Round: Swim with fistgloves®. Just swim at your previous effort, not trying to hit any particular count. How many strokes above your ungloved spl are you?

2nd Round: Swim without fistgloves®. Without particularly trying, but simply letting the fistglove® experience affect you naturally, compare your stroke counts to your previous spl, both with and without gloves.

SL Exercise #5

Swim 100+75+50+25.

Repeat Exercise #2 but this time, maintain the spl from your 100 at every shorter distance. If your 100 is @ 72 strokes for an N of 18 spl, your goal is to take exactly 54-36-18 for 75-50-25. Here are several possibilities for this set:

1.   You find it difficult to "fit in" all the prescribed strokes as you swim shorter distances.

2.   You can fit them in, but you feel a bit ragged or hurried, trying to take that many strokes on the 50 or 25.

3.   You find yourself, *without any noticeable increase in effort*, able to simply swim faster as your distance decreases.

This is a particularly valuable exercise. If you succeed and #3 happens, you've just learned how to hold your SL consistent (constant spl of 18 spl) yet increase your SR (i.e., you swam faster with constant SL; if V increases, then SR must have increased.)

SL Exercise #6

Swim 4 rounds of 4 x 25 (16 total laps).

Take the lowest and highest spl from Exercise #1 and in each round, swim 1 x 25 at each count. If your count for 25 was 15 spl and you took 72 strokes (18 spl) on the 100, swim the four rounds in these counts:

1st Round: 15-16-17-18
2nd Round: 18-17-16-15
3rd Round: 15-16-17-18
4th Round: 18-17-16-15

On the first two rounds, simply focus on *calibrating* your SL. See how finely and accurately you can adjust your stroke and timing to hit the wall in exactly the prescribed count, with no end-of-lap adjusting. You'll discover that the puzzle of subtracting strokes (2nd and 4th Rounds) is entirely different from that of adding strokes (1st and 3rd Rounds). If you were reasonably adept at calibrating and adjusting your SL on the first two rounds, then see if you can swim a bit faster on the third and fourth. If not, then your task is just to calibrate better on the final two rounds.

SL Builders

The SL exercises have allowed you to begin learning your stroke-count range and how distance or speed may affect it. The next step in Effective Training is to apply that knowledge in sets that combine aerobic and neuromuscular training. The aerobic effects come from swimming longer sets. The neuromuscular training — the more beneficial effect — will teach you to maintain a longer stroke for a longer duration, which is precisely how to be successful when you swim an actual race. SL Builders give you an organized way to develop that capacity. Here's how they make you a better swimmer:

1. They systematically increase your SL and gradually lower your stroke-count range.

2. They help you practice keeping your SL consistent as you increase distance or speed, or decrease your rest intervals. This gives you a type of control characteristic of the world's best swimmers.

Our starting point is a 600-yard set, slightly longer than the quarter-mile swim that is common in sprint triathlons but long enough to test your ability to maintain SL for a medium distance. For purposes of illustration, I'll use an "N" of 16 spl, but in doing the sets, choose your own N, based on your experiences from SL exercises. And note that any N you choose doesn't mean that you need to swim that stroke count on *every* length. The N will be the average spl for the distance you swim. For 50 in 32 strokes, you might go 15+17. For 75 in 48 strokes, you might go 15+16+17. For 100 in 64 strokes: 15+16+16+17. And so on.

Start Here:
What: Swim 12 x 50 (12 repeats of 50 yards). Rest for at least 5 yoga breaths between swims.

How: Swimming with attention (but not attempting *perfection*), count your strokes for the first 50. Your only goal is to not exceed that count (i.e., 32 in our example) on #s 2 through 12. That may be easy enough for the first few repeats but, at some point, you may take your 32nd stroke a few yards from the wall. If so, roll to your Sweet Spot and kick easily the rest of the way. Now you're on notice: *It will take discipline to hold your SL.* You'll have to focus on how you *spend* each stroke. Before long, you'll naturally start employing strategies for making your target count. You'll realize that to complete 50 yards in 32 strokes, you probably should do the first 25 in 15…and perhaps that you need to pass the mid-pool marker in 6 strokes to finish the first 25 in 15. This kind of hyper-alertness is a big step toward developing SL vigilance.

Benefit: In conventional workouts, where you race the pace clock or other swimmers, you'd probably take more and shorter strokes as you strain to keep up or make intervals — not a good signal to send your nervous system. *SL Builders* teach you to maintain consistent SL, even as you tire, and to block out distractions that would normally cause you to lose efficiency.

The Next Step
The first few times you attempt this set, don't be surprised if you have to ease off a bit in mid-set to avoid increasing your stroke count. Don't let that faze you! Speed isn't the immediate goal; developing the discipline to hold a slightly challenging SL is. Let's say you've been swimming for years

with an average stroke count of 20 spl but are now diligently working at holding 16 spl. Until your nervous system adapts to the new SL, it's entirely normal to sacrifice a little SR and V (from the formula V = SL x SR) to do so. Whenever I've established a new PR for my 100-yard stroke count, I have to swim super slowly to achieve it, but I always rebuild that speed steadily over a few weeks. You'll do the same. So here are the steps in mastering your Level 1 Stroke Builder.

1.   Do this set once or twice a week. At first, just get used to completing 600 yards in 50-yard increments @ 32 strokes (or whatever target count you choose) with no regard for speed.

2.   As the new SL begins to feel a bit more natural (this means your neuromuscular system is adapting), you'll find you can maintain a more consistent speed, maybe even go a bit faster on the last two or three repeats. This means your body is figuring out how to keep SL and SR consistent for an extended set of swims. *This is a hugely important skill of successful distance swimming!*

3.   As you become comfortable swimming with your new, improved SL, you can make the set a bit more challenging in several ways:

- **Increase the duration.** Add a few repeats, perhaps up to 16 reps.
- **Decrease your rest interval.** If you've been resting for 5 breaths between swims, see if you can swim the last few reps just as well on a 4-breath rest. When that seems easy, extend that rest interval earlier into the set. Then try a 3-breath rest in the same way.
- **Swim just a bit faster on the last few reps, and then a few more.** Always add speed bit-by-bit from the end of the set. This will develop the habit of getting stronger, rather than slower, as you go.
- **Don't try, just yet, to reduce your spl or N.** Instead, take the time to make this new, improved SL a no-brainer, almost boring in its ease. When that happens, you're ready for Step 3 and that is...

Swim 8 X 75 on a 5-breath rest interval, all at 48 or fewer strokes.

This is a 600-yard set, the same as our initial SL Builder set, but with only 8 breaks for rest, rather than 12. You're moving incrementally closer to swimming 600 straight. The goal is to continue maintaining the original N of 16 spl (or the target count you chose.) The same rules apply as for the 50s. First learn to complete the set without exceeding 48 strokes per 75...then to complete the set at consistent speed/effort...then to reduce your rest interval by one breath, then two...then to swim the last few reps just a bit stronger...then to add reps, up to about 12 x 75. And so on. There's no hard and fast rule for how to make the set more challenging. You have three variables: how many reps, how fast, how much rest. You decide how to add difficulty; just continue to take an organized approach.

You will follow this process in gradually moving toward a long swim done without rest in the spl that, at first, was challenging to maintain on 50-yard repeats. The steps you can follow are fairly straightforward: 6 to 12 x 100, 4 to 8 x 150, 3 to 6 x 200, 2 to 4 x 300 and finally a straight swim of 600 to 1200 yards, all of it at 16 spl. When you reach the end of the process (and don't rush it; give yourself several weeks), it should be a breeze to swim a significant distance in a consistent, efficient SL and at a consistent speed, perhaps even picking up a bit of speed at the end.

When you achieve that, *and only then*, it's time to choose a new, lower spl and start the process all over again, with a set of 12 to 16 repeats of 50 yards. After successfully completing your first cycle of this disciplined, orderly, distance-building progression, you may find yourself able to move through the steps at the new stroke count more smoothly. Most important, you have taken yourself out of the frustrating cycle of pointless lap marathons that accomplish nothing good for your swimming. And you're ready to add some other skills and challenges to your Effective Training, most importantly the ability to "shift gears" while swimming.

How Fast?

In the SL-Builder sets, we added speed as one of our goals for the first time. That can be a bit of a distraction to a swimmer who should be working mainly on increasing efficiency. Speed is a relative term. I've mentioned several times that the smartest thing you can do to improve your total race time is to swim easier, not faster. Faster times should virtually always be a natural product of greater efficiency. Practicing efficiency is the smartest way to make speed happen — the kind of speed that's easy to maintain for long distances with little effort.

One of the best ways to make speed happen is to avoid timing yourself. At least in the beginning. I've recommended that you ignore the pace clock in setting rest intervals. Well keep ignoring it — and that cherished sports watch on your wrist — as you aim to add a little speed to your repeats. Here's a radical idea: instead of checking your watch, just *feel* your speed. As an athlete who has done a fair amount of various kinds of training, you should have a well-calibrated internal speedometer. You may not know the *exact* speed, but you can tell relative speed by feel.

On the SL-Builder sets and on other sets in Chapter 15, whenever I mention adding speed as one of your goals, see if you can do that strictly by feel, at least a few times, before you refer to pace clock or sports watch for confirmation, or an exact measure of how much faster you may have gotten. There are at least two benefits to doing so:

1. Better focus. For inexperienced swimmers, the pace clock can be a serious distraction, a source of pressure that can break down the focus and discipline needed to allow new habits of efficiency and fluency to develop.

2. Better self-knowledge. There are no pace clocks along the route — and it's pretty hard to check your watch — when you swim the races you're training for. Doing descending sets strictly by feel, on a regular basis, is a good way to help you develop your internal pace clock.

Later, after you've begun to use the pace clock a bit more regularly and have begun to add times to your stroke-count data base, make it a regular practice to "guess" your time for a repeat as you're finishing, before you look at the clock. A successful distance swimmer can predict his or her repeat time within a very close margin and then swim that time almost on command. Or…adjust her prediction as she swims, based on how she feels. Learning to swim without the clock and then to use it judiciously will help you develop the "clock-in-the-head" knack yourself.

Chapter 15

Gears: You Learn the Easiest Way to Swim Faster

I f you took a track cycle out on a hilly road course — without a set of gears to help you go up and down economically — your thighs would be toast in no time. If you drove your car in only one gear, you'd burn out your engine in a hurry...*and* limit your speed dramatically. And yet, virtually every swimmer has only one "gear" for swimming — mainly because they swim most of the time in such a narrow range of SL/SR combinations that their nervous system is not adaptable to anything else. This is true even for many competitive swimmers. Accomplished distance swimmers feel disorganized if they try to sprint, because their nervous systems practice swimming movements only at a Stroke Rate between 60 and 80 strokes per minute, while sprinting happens at upwards of 100 strokes per minute. This chapter will guide you through practice that will give you a set of swimming gears good for any triathlon. They'll allow you to adjust a race plan, to discover the easiest way to swim at the speeds you choose, and to make training more interesting and fun as they give you an unusually complete skill set.

Up to this point, drills and mindful swimming, in the Learning and Practice modes, have given you the balance and coordination to find your optimal Stroke Length. SL Exercises and SL Builders have helped you to begin refining the best range of stroke counts (spl) for practice, and to systematically increase your SL. The next level of Effective Training is similar to a piano student playing hours of simple notes, chords, and scales until he becomes so deft in striking the right keys that his playing moves from *conscious* to *unconscious* competence. These exercises will first teach you to "play" SL and stroke counts as easily as a pianist playing scales and then help you use your developing gears to learn how to build speed almost effortlessly.

Develop Your Swimming "Gears"

In all these set examples, I will use, for purpose of illustration, an N of 16 spl. You must find and choose your own N. Sometimes that may change from day to day, depending on how fatigued you may be from other training. Remember: your N is usually an average. On a 75-yard repeat, an N of 16 means you aim for 48 total strokes, which might be 15+16+17.

First Gear: Simple Gear Changing

Swim 4 rounds of 5 x 25. Rest for 3 to 5 yoga breaths or bobs between swims.

We did a set like this in the SL Exercises, but we'll repeat it as a tune-up, as a piano student might warm up by playing scales. Using an N of 16, we'll start at N-2 (14 spl), then swim at N-1 (15 spl), then at N, then N+1 (17 spl), then N+2 (18 spl) on the first round, reverse that order on the second round, then repeat those two rounds.

In other words, the set looks like this:

1st Round: @ **14-15-16-17-18**
2nd Round: @ **18-17-16-15-14**
3rd Round: @ **14-15-16-17-18**
4th Round: @ **18-17-16-15-14**

The first two rounds are a test of how well you can *calibrate* your SL. See how finely and accurately you can adjust your stroke and timing to hit the wall in exactly the prescribed count, with no end-of-lap adjusting. The puzzle of subtracting strokes (2nd Round) will turn out to be a completely different task than that of adding strokes (1st Round). The second puzzle is how to be smooth and seamless at both ends of the scale. Can you swim the lowest stroke count without losing rhythm, without a looong pushoff? Can you swim the highest stroke count without getting choppy or rushed?

On the first two rounds, your learning curve may be steep. But the final two rounds are for applying what you learned solving those puzzles earlier in the set. Calibrate better and be more fluent from the lowest to the highest stroke count. If you pass both tests and want to add one more challenge, do the scale, up and down, one more time and see how fast you can swim at each stroke count. What's the fastest 25 you can swim @ 14 strokes — and at every other count as you move up the scale and back down again? When putting more emphasis on speed, do two things: (1) Just *feel* it, don't time it and (2) take as much rest as you want between swims. But most of all, have *fun* with these puzzles.

Second Gear: Intermediate Gear Changing

To continue our piano-playing analogy for "playing" Stroke Length, we'll take the SL just practiced with 25-yard repeats and put together some "chords" with 50s and 75s, to heighten our ability to calibrate SL and change it "on the fly." This will develop a capacity for adaptability that improves your skill set and also serves as a rehearsal for changing speeds efficiently in a race.

Swim 2 or more rounds of 4 x 50 with the following stroke counts (or your own chosen spl combinations):

1st 50: 14+15
2nd 50: 15+16
3rd 50: 16+17
4th 50: 17+18

Don't time your 50s when you first practice this set. You first task is to calibrate your SL, to get comfortable with hitting the prescribed count on each length. The second step is to stay smooth and fluent at every stroke count. Do as many rounds as you want, as long as it feels good and remains interesting to do it, until you have developed a keen feel for changing SL on the fly. For rest intervals, take as many yoga breaths as you need to feel ready to nail the target stroke counts on the next swim. Allow a bit of extra recovery between rounds by doing 100 to 200 yards of your favorite drills. (When you become truly effortless on this, you won't need any extra rest between rounds.) Once you're in a "flow state" on these — and this may take a week or more of 50-yard practice — move up to 75-yard repeats as shown below.

Swim 2 or more rounds of 3 x 75 with stroke counts sequenced as follows:

1st 75: 14+15+16
2nd 75: 15+16+17
3rd 75: 16+17+18

Solve this new puzzle in the same way you previously solved the 50-yard puzzle. Your goal is to continue mindfully, patiently, purposefully repeating sets like these in practice until you can practically do them in your sleep and smoothly hit any stroke count in your range at will...and feel controlled and fluent at all combinations.

Finally, if you find all of this almost boringly easy to do, here's a challenge that is guaranteed to put your SL adaptability to a severe test. Do the 50s or 75s in reverse order. In other words, like this:

1st 75: 18+17+16
2nd 75: 17+16+15
3rd 75: 16+15+14

Good luck on this one. You'll need it, but if you can do this successfully, you're ready for promotion to the Life Master level of using your swimming gears.

Third Gear: Advanced Gear Changing

The exercises above have given you an introductory course in how to use your gears, so you can move somewhat adeptly around your stroke-count range. If you've done these successfully, you're ready to use your gears on a "hilly course," by which I mean changing repeat distances and more frequent gear changes. These sets will help you maximize what you can do in combining SL and SR in all kinds of sets from silent and super slow to racing speeds, and will teach you to use lower counts at slower speeds to "set you up" for greater efficiency at higher speeds. For races, this will specifically prepare you to start at a relaxed pace, to find your most efficient "groove" for a pace you can sustain effortlessly at any distance, and then, if you choose, to efficiently speed up, perhaps to leapfrog from a slower-moving pack to a faster one, or to accelerate briefly to pass another swimmer.

Begin this 1000-yard set by swimming 1 x 100 at a moderate effort (say, 75%). Count your total strokes then divide by 4 to calculate your average spl. In this example, we'll assume a total stroke count of 64, which will give us an N of 16 spl. Then use your N in the following way (stroke counts in parentheses are from the example of 16 spl)

Swim 4 rounds of (3 X 25)
Each round of 25s is N–2, N-1, N (14, 15, 16)
Swim 2 rounds of (3 X 50)
Each round of 50s is N–2, N-1, N (28, 30, 32)
Swim 1 round of (4 X 75)
Each 75 is N-2 + N-1 + N (14+15+16 or 45 total strokes)

Here's what you'll probably experience as you go through the set: On the first round of 25s you'll probably just be calibrating your stroke length. In each successive round, as you calibrate a bit more finely, you'll change gears with more of an effortless flow, and — just as would be the case if you change gears more adeptly on your bicycle — you'll probably swim a bit faster. This experience results in two key benefits: First, neuromuscular learning occurs as your brain processes new information on each of the 12 lengths in that set. Second, you learn to swim faster without swimming any harder. You use efficiency rather than effort to accelerate, and that will be a priceless lesson.

The same learning experience will be repeated on the two rounds of 50s and the set of 75s, except with your motor-learning center being challenged at a slightly higher degree of complexity each time. Not only does the puzzle change every length, but also you tackle a higher-order puzzle after each cycle of 300 yards.

Continue using yoga breaths or bobs for your rest interval, perhaps adding a breath or two to your rest period as you move from 25s to 50s to 75s for your repeat distance. If you like, insert 100 or 200 of your favorite drill (or swimming with an SSP focal point) as recovery between rounds of 300; before long, you'll be able to move easily from round to round, changing gears and speeds as easily in the water as you do on your bike in the course of a 10-mile ride. Continue, at least initially, to ignore the pace clock. Simply *feel* your speed develop naturally as you let yourself "rev it up" a bit by adding strokes from lap to lap.

Fourth Gear: Lance Armstrong in the Water

If you've gotten this far, you are already swimming with an assurance and mastery enjoyed by only a tiny fraction of all swimmers on earth. You're now ready for graduate-level gear changing.

In the examples below, start the set by swimming a moderate-effort 100 to find your N for the rest of the set. Take your total stroke count, divide by four, and use that as your N to calculate your target stroke counts for all the repeats that follow. Most important, in this set, the N is an *average* stroke count for each swim. There is no prescribed stroke count for each length within a swim. If your target count for the 75s is N-1 (which is 15 spl or 45 total strokes in the examples I've chosen), you can take the 45 strokes as 15+15+15 or 14+15+16…or 16+15+14, for that matter. With repeated practice, you'll soon know the easiest and most efficient way to hit your stroke counts for any speed or effort.

Swim 2 rounds of 500 as follows

1st Round:

> 1 x 100 @ N (64 strokes)
> 2 x 75 @ N-1 (45 strokes)
> 3 x 50 @ N-2 (28 strokes)
> 4 x 25 @ N (16 strokes)

Active Rest: 100 Drill or Silent Swim, then:

2nd Round

> 1 x 100 @ N-2 (56 strokes)
> 2 x 75 @ N-1 (45 strokes)
> 3 x 50 @ N (32 strokes)
> 4 x 25 @ N-2 (14 strokes)

Let's examine what you'll likely experience in the course of each set and the learning that results. You start with an easily achievable stroke count in the 1st Round. As you move to the 75s, the spl gets a bit more challenging, but the repeat is shorter. The 50s offer the same combination of tougher spl with easier repeat distance. In each set, you're also practicing the calibrate-and-recalibrate skill again. The 2nd 75 should go more smoothly than the first. Ditto for the last two 50s. But when you get to the 25s, suddenly the spl gets bumped back up to the starting point. The combination of easier spl *and* easier repeat distance means you may "run out of pool" before taking the allotted number of strokes. So your task on the 25s is to learn to *fit in* the added strokes smoothly, which means to swim fast fluently.

After the first round, give yourself a recovery 100 of drilling or an SSP, if you like, then tackle the second 500. On the second round you'll use the same range of stroke counts, but the task — and the learning experience — will be completely different: You'll start with the longest repeat and lowest spl. You'll have to swim with incredible discipline and mindfulness to finish the 100 @ N-2. (Remember an average of 14 spl could be done as 13+14+14+15, for instance.) But then you *add* strokes as the repeat distance gets shorter on the 75s and 50s. The 50s @ N should be a breeze and you should be able to do them with a nice feeling of *easy speed*. When you get to the 25s @ N-2, you're back to "stroke deprivation," needing to subtract two strokes per length from your count on the 50s. *But*, because they're 25s, try to swim them **as fast as possible** in the allotted 14 strokes. If you get to the point where you can do all this successfully, Congratulations! You have just crammed as much learning as is humanly possible into 1000 yards of swimming. You've also done a lot more to develop your swimming and triathlon potential than one more "same old, same old" set of generic 100-yard repeats on 2:00, or 1:30 or even 1:10.

The above set makes use of the world's most incredible learning machine — the human brain and body. The most neglected ingredient in training — for virtually all athletes, not just triathletes — is that of "fooling the body." The whole point of training is to create adaptability. Give the body a task it has not done before and it adapts by making changes to strengthen its ability to successfully complete the task. Running, cycling, or swimming farther or faster stimulates your body to make cell-level energy-system changes to be equal to the task. Once it has made those changes, however, doing the same set again will not produce further adaptation. Yet most athletes do the same sets in the same way, day after day, week after week, year after year, motivated by the desire to "top off" the fuel tank.

Effective Training sets keep your brain, body, and neuromuscular system in a state of *confusion*, having to constantly come up with solutions to new puzzles and tasks. And the more continually you maintain an environment for *adaptability*, the greater the *capability* you create.

Swimming for Time: Speed at Last

U p to now, we've ignored the pace clock — something verging on heresy among swimmers and coaches. But we've had good reason: Allowing you to fully develop swimming as an *art* has readied you to train for it as a *sport* with far greater return for your investment of precious time and energy. With stroke count now ingrained as your most important piece of training data, we'll finally begin using the pace clock to give you another piece of information to cross-reference with your stroke-count numbers. This will give you the complete swimming-improvement picture. We'll start with my favorite pool game: Swimming Golf.

Swimming Golf

To play Swimming Golf, count your strokes for a fixed, short distance (I prefer 50s because the math is manageable) and add your time in seconds to that number. This gives you a structured way to find your most economical SL and tempo. For any swimming speed, there are many potential combinations of SL and SR; from one extreme of a very short stroke with extremely high turnover to a very looong stroke with a very slooow turnover. Neither extreme is energy-efficient, but playing Swim Golf and experimenting with a variety of combinations helps you quickly pinpoint the one that works best for you. And when you compare your effort level with your score, you gain an accurate measure of how to produce the greatest V with the least expenditure of energy. By playing regularly, you find the smartest, easiest way to the lowest score, using cunning rather than muscle. Here are examples of the two basic ways to lower your score. Please don't be intimidated by the stroke counts, times, and scores that you see here. Remember: Swim Golf is relative. No matter what your starting "score," (and it might be 90, 100, 110 or more), the point is to lower that score. You'll see benefits no matter what your starting point.

Version 1: On successive 50s, swim the same time but reduce your stroke count.

Example:
    32 total strokes + :50 = 82
    31 total strokes + :50 = 81
    30 total strokes + :50 = 80
In this example, you'd start by swimming a relaxed 50 in 50 seconds. Adding your count of 32 strokes to your time yields a score of 82. The goal in this version is to repeat the same time on each succeeding 50 in the set, but to continue subtracting strokes, until you can't shave any more from your count without sacrificing speed.

This makes for an intriguing puzzle. You could, for instance, subtract a stroke by holding a longer glide after your pushoff, but that will slow you down a bit, so you'd need to regain that time without adding back the stroke you saved on your pushoff. The most valuable learning experience will come from using the knowledge you gained in Chapter 15 to carve strokes from your total, but — each time — to add just a little bit more "oomph" to each remaining stroke to keep your time the same. This version will teach you a lot; have fun with it.

Version 2: On successive 50s, maintain your stroke count, but descend your time.

Example:

30 total strokes + :45 = 75

30 total strokes + :44 = 74

30 total strokes + :43 = 73

In this example, you swim at a chosen stroke count, then note your time from the pace clock after finishing. To improve your score you need to keep exactly the same stroke length, but *take each stroke just a bit faster* in order to shave time. This poses a different problem and a different learning experience than the previous version. Looking at this version in light of the formula **V = SL x SR**, what you must do here is increase V (i.e., go faster) by raising your SR while keeping SL the same. It's not easy, but as soon as you begin solving it, you've advanced your skill set to an exceptionally high order by acquiring the knack that decides races at the Olympics.

Your improving golf score will provide an unerring measure of how well you're using SL to create speed. If you play regularly, you'll be amazed at how quickly a bit more effort can add a lot more strokes. If those strokes don't translate into enough speed to lower your total score, you know right away you've been wasteful and can take quick steps to fix the problem.

Swimming Golf sets and scores are also the perfect way to develop a kinesthetic sense of how you should feel at the beginning of any swim longer than 400 meters in racing or as you start longer training sets. When you record a personal best score, immediately capture and store how you felt while swimming it. Those that feel the easiest, yet produce a solid score, give you a benchmark for the kind of stroke sensations you should aim for in your races. With enough practice, you'll be able to put yourself in a flow state at will.

Tiger Woods in the Water

Once you have the basics of Swimming Golf, you can easily add refinements to raise your game to a higher level. The first step is to begin factoring in your heart rate or Rate of Perceived Exertion (RPE; see Chapter 12). You may play Swimming Golf inefficiently at first, wearing yourself out to get a good score. For example, you may drop your score by kicking harder, something you couldn't sustain in a long race or training swim.

The advanced golfer measures her scores against the effort needed to achieve them. If you swam a 50 in 32 strokes and 37 seconds for a 69 score, but had an RPE of 5, you'd be hard-pressed to swim like that for more than one or two 50s — and would probably need to rest a minute or more between them. On the other hand, when you can swim that 69 score with an RPE of 3, you might be able to maintain it for 10 to 20 repeats, perhaps resting only 3 to 5 yoga breaths between swims; this would definitely be a "race-ready" golf score.

Thus, reducing your RPE at a particular score is just as useful a goal as lowering that score. You might save energy by swimming more efficiently, or you might do it by using a different strokes/seconds combination. The more curious and creative you are in playing, the more you'll learn. Here are several variations that will make you a "tour golfer:"

1.   Do a round of 3 to 4 x 50s to establish a benchmark score. Then do several rounds with fistgloves®. How close can you come to your ungloved scores? Finally, remove the gloves and do another round ungloved. Does your ungloved score improve after "educating" your hands with the gloves? If so, capture and store the feeling it produces.

2.   How many ways can you score? Tiger Woods is so dominant because he has shots in his repertoire that other golfers can barely imagine. Once you've been playing for a while and have established your own "par," test how many different stroke counts you can swim at a slightly higher score. For example, if your record score is 77, try swimming a series at a constant score of 80 as shown below.

30 strokes + :50
31 strokes + :49
32 strokes + :48
33 strokes + :47
34 strokes + :46

At the end of the series, identify which combination felt easiest. That goes into your muscle "memory bank."

3. Repeat short series of 50s at several stroke counts. E.g., If you have an N of 20 spl (or 40 strokes per 50), try several rounds of 50s as follows:

3 x 50 @ 38 strokes
3 x 50 @ 39 strokes
3 x 50 @ 40 strokes
3 x 50 @ 41 strokes

Descend your golf score on each round and compare your best scores. Which stroke count produced the best combination of low score and low RPE? File that away. Want to learn even more? Occasionally, swim either of those series in the reverse order, from higher count to lower. The same range of counts will produce fresh insights, when you subtract, rather than adding, strokes.

4. Different Strokes. As the TI video *Freestyle and Backstroke: The Total Immersion Way* demonstrated, alternating backstroke and freestyle can benefit both strokes, more than practicing either one alone. I particularly enjoy doing Long-Axis Combinations in Swimming Golf. Here's one of my favorite series. I may do two or three rounds of the following:

3 to 4 x 50s backstroke. Count strokes and take times. Aim for best score.
3 to 4 x 50s (25 backstroke + 25 freestyle). As above.
3 to 4 x 50s freestyle. As above.

Compare the score you achieve for freestyle after swimming backstroke and then back/free as a warmup, against scores you achieve in other types of sets. Want to learn still more? Do a round of the above with fistgloves®, then another round with "nekked hands."

5. Use your own experiences to create imaginative golf sets to measure any aspect of your swimming. Try doing golf sets Super Slow and compare them with your scores at, say, 70%, 80% and 90% effort. Do them as silently as you can or with a focus on Piercing the Water and compare your scores with those you achieve using other focal points. Any "tweak" that produces a better score or the same score with a lower RPE is useful. File it away for use in a race or in another training set.

No More Generic Training

With so many learning experiences from TI Lessons and thoughtful whole-stroke sets filed in your body's "athletic-performance hard-drive" you now have the tools to transform the generic sets prescribed in any book, article, or Masters workout, into Effective Training. Here's one simple example, based on a fairly routine training set.

The coach or magazine article prescribes a set of **5 x 100**. You can choose any of the following ways of doing it.

Option 1: Swim all 5 x 100 at the same time and same stroke count. You're practicing constant SL, SR, and V.

Option 2: Swim all 5 x 100 in the same time, but subtract one stroke from each successive repeat. You're practicing constant V, but producing it more with SL and less with SR.

Option 3: Swim all 5 x 100 in the same stroke count, but descend your time on each repeat. Same SL, but more V from gradually increasing SR.

Option 4: Swim 5 x 100, adding one stroke to each successive repeat and descend your time. You go faster by "trading" some SL for more SR. This option offers other choices you can make in where to trade that SL for more V to practice yet-finer control.

In this example, speed and SR are added to the end of the repeat first, while maintaining the initial SL at the beginning of each repeat until deep into the set — which is smart rehearsal for effective distance racing:

Example:
- **13+14+14+15 = 56**
- **13+14+14+16 = 57**
- **13+14+15+16 = 58**
- **13+15+15+16 = 59**
- **14+15+15+16 = 60**

Each of these examples would slightly change the learning experience and training effect of what was once a pretty generic training set. And each such change would squeeze out a bit more adaptation value from a finite amount of training time.

A need for speed?

The training program I have suggested will thoroughly prepare 95 percent of all triathletes for unprecedented racing success. But a small number, those seeking to race at a near-elite level or above (not just pro's but top age-groupers too) may have more specialized requirements. Particularly in races where drafting on the bike is legal, medals are often substantially decided by the swim finish. So, for a small number of triathletes, it may be critically important to splash out of the water with the lead pack.

Many triathletes have prepared themselves for that by doing "anaerobic swimming" or simply *going hard*. The goal is to tolerate the pain of lactic acid buildup. Admittedly not much fun and, I think, perhaps not all that necessary even for elites. Ivar Brinkman, a TI-trained triathlon coach in Belgium, has his athletes do about 10 percent of their total swimming yardage in sprints, usually in combination with longer swims, mainly to rehearse for the experience of sprinting the first part of the swim leg, to get in the draft of the fastest swimmers, then settling into a more sustainable pace.

One of his favored sets is 2 to 3 rounds of (4 x 50 + 1 x 200). The 50s are done quite briskly on a rest interval of perhaps 15 seconds. The 200s are done at about 80 percent of maximum. To include a TI emphasis, try to maintain a consistent SL on the fast 50s and a slightly lower count, perhaps one less stroke-per-length, on the 200s. Ivar also has his athletes do some fast 25s or 50s at the end of practice, to mimic the race finish. You can easily apply any of the stroke-count suggestions in the last two chapters to these sets.

And a particularly instructive way of practicing sprinting — or *swimming fast*, as I prefer to call it — is to mix slower and faster cycles on the same lap. One of my favorite ways of doing so is to swim 8 to 12 x 50s, swimming the first 6 or 8 strokes (3 to 4 cycles) of each length with great SL (as if trying to complete the lap in a very low stroke count) and then shifting to a high SR for the rest of the lap. Do the best job you can of preserving your SL as you do. Bottom line though, swim smart and you'll be far better prepared for any race.

Chapter 17

Swimming for Distance: Focus on Economy, Not Conditioning

I don't know which was harder for Alice: betting a friend they'd both finally do a triathlon or asking my advice on how to train. She's done just fine on her own in cycling and running, doing rides of up to 50 miles with a local bike club, and running semi-regularly for 25 years, lining up for a road race now and again. And she's a reasonably good swimmer, with fine technique from years of practicing TI drills. But the thought of having to swim a quarter mile across open water before she ever gets near her bike has stopped her in her tracks when it comes to triathlon.

But the bet changed all that because she let me put her on a program that can take the teeth out of the quarter-mile swim for anybody. Instead of attacking the distance all at once, as if it was the Matterhorn, you break it up into a lot of manageable hills over several weeks. By race day, almost without noticing what you've done, you're ready.

Alice's story is typical of many would-be first-time triathletes. She swims anywhere from a half mile to a mile at the pool, one or two lengths at a time. Does this count, she wonders? Can 50-yard repeats get you ready for a straight swim of 500 yards in the pool, much less in open water, where there won't be a reassuring wall every 25 yards? Well, yes, at least as the first rung. And 50-yard repeats can help get you ready for a triathlon swim of any distance — even up to the 2.4-mile swim that begins a full Ironman. If you've swum only short distances and wonder how to build up to a non-stop quarter-mile or more, this chapter presents a plan for using short swims as building blocks to get there. We'll begin with a plan for short distances (400 to 500 yards), and then present one that can be adapted for longer swims of from 1 to 2.4 miles.

Training Program for a Short Triathlon Swim

What Alice needs in order to prepare for a quarter-mile swim is a ladder strategy, a pool training program that will build both her repeat distances and her confidence, step by step, by gradually and systematically stretching the distance she swims between rest breaks in her workouts.

After covering a quarter-mile straight (something that only an estimated 2 percent of all swimmers can do, by the way), we'll throw in a little speed to make sure her bicycle isn't the last one racked in the transition area when she hits the beach on D-Day. Because she has already done 10 years of technique-oriented swimming, her stroke is already fairly good (consistently holding 15 to 16 spl), and we can place more emphasis on swimming in her program. (You should stay mainly with drill-based practices and drill/swim practices until you can keep your spl within about 10 percent of your base as distance increases.)

To gradually build from 50-yard repeats to her target distance, Alice will use a single, timed, 500-yard set each workout. It won't be the only thing she does, but it will become a main set for specific race prep in each workout. She'll add another 1200 to 1500 yards to reach her normal workout yardage, which she can do with a variety of Practice-type sets (including warm-up) before and after the 500 set.

Everything is based on her total elapsed time, both swimming and resting, for the set. She can take as much rest as she needs between each repeat at first, but she'll work on gradually reducing it to "zero" rest — the same amount she'll be entitled to on race day. For example, if she does ten 50-yard repeats in 60 seconds each, and rests an average of 15 seconds every time, her total time for the set will be 12 and a half minutes. As her stamina grows and she later swims ten 50s at the same speed, but with only 10 seconds rest between, her time will drop to 11:40.

The key is making individual swims gradually longer and subtracting rest periods. That alone will improve her times. The 500-yard main set gets done at least once a week, and she will remain at each level until she feels comfortable moving to the next, or until her time for the set no longer improves. Once she tops out at the straight 500-yard swim, she can shift to an emphasis on gaining speed by going back to any of the first five levels to practice swimming at slightly higher speeds, while maintaining at least the same SL.

Quarter-Mile Countdown

Your goal is to make your swims longer without noticeably increasing the effort. A plateau on any level means it's time to go to the next one. All distances are in either yards or meters.

- **10 x 50**
- **75-50-75-50-75-50-75-50**
- **100-100-75-75-50-50-50**
- **5 x 100**
- **200-150-100-50**
- **250-125-125**
- **250-250**
- **300-200**
- **400-100**
- **500**

This training program could easily be expanded if you are preparing for a sprint-triathlon swim of up to one-half mile. You could adjust the distances to either 10 X 100 or 20 X 50. For swims of more than one-half mile, you should use the following training program.

Training Program for a Long Triathlon Swim

Instinct tells many triathletes that the only way to get ready for a long swim is with sheer yardage and long swims. So they plod grimly through pool marathons. It's boring, sure, but at least you know that if you can keep your arms going long enough to finish, you've got a better chance in the race. But no amount of training can compensate for energy lost to inefficient stroking. For any swimmer whose skill level isn't pretty high, generic volume-based workouts will do nothing more than imprint slow, inefficient swimming.

To maximize your potential in any triathlon with a swim of more than one-half mile, you have to be able to swim almost effortlessly. The opportunity to misspend heartbeats you'll need to bike for 25 to 112 miles and run anywhere from 5K to a marathon is astronomical. Considering how few of the total miles you'll cover in a triathlon are devoted to swimming, the watery leg often consumes an extravagant amount of the energy available for the whole race. Unless you swam on a very high competitive level in a former athletic life (think Sheila Taormina), your smartest goal on the swim leg is to exit the water with a low heart rate. And your swim training should be devoted almost exclusively to practicing economy.

The swimming leg — though it may seem long — is too short for a speedier swim, by itself, to make a significant difference in a race that will last anywhere from two and a half to twelve hours or more. In an Ironman, for example, if you pick up five or ten minutes by swimming harder, that effort can easily cost you an hour or more back on land. But gains in efficiency and economy may not only shave 10 to 30 minutes from your Ironman swim distance, but possibly also produce *substantial* time drops for the rest of the race, simply because you'll be much fresher entering the first transition. We've received reports from many Total Immersion alums that this is *precisely* what happened to them in a race.

So your first goal is to gain the freedom to swim as easily as you wish — to be able to virtually float through the swim leg if you choose. The key is to train yourself to maintain a relaxed, low-drag, fluent stroke for distances that gradually increase to the length of the swim in your chosen race. Unless you're among the elites, swimming *speed* is simply not important. Swimming *ease* is the non-negotiable skill. Here's a program to get it, and then keep it as you gradually increase your training yardage. It's based on shorter-distance repeats, which I use as the "meat" of my own training for open-water races at distances from 1 to 6 miles. This program assumes that you are training for an Ironman swim of 2.4 miles. If you are training for a half-Ironman swim of 1.2 miles, you could adjust the program by starting with, say, 10 X 100 and then, at weeks #5, 8, 10, 11, and 12, increase the number of 100s by 2 instead of by 5. If you do this, you would be swimming 20 X 100 in the final week. Similarly, if you are training for a swim of 1000 yards or meters, you could begin the program with 5 X 100 and, at weeks #5, 8, 10, 11, and 12, increase the number of 100s by 1, so that you are swimming 1000 yards in the final week.

1. Measure your efficiency. Start by doing a relaxed nonstop swim of 15 to 20 minutes (5 to 10 minutes or 10 to 15 minutes, respectively, if you are training for a swim of 1000 yards or a mile) to gauge your ability to swim at a steady pace with constant efficiency. Start about as slowly as you can go without it becoming a drill and see if you can sustain that pace (perhaps even pick it up a bit in the last minute or two) without working noticeably harder as laps go by. At the same time, count your spl at any time in the first 200. Recheck your count every 6 to 8 lengths. Can you maintain your stroke efficiency within 10% of your lowest count? (i.e., if your first count was 20, no subsequent lap exceeds 22.) If so, you're ready to begin some longer training swims.

2. Make flow and economy a habit. Don't worry about how far or fast for a while. Focus instead on "how right." Swim a regular main set (twice a week) of 15 x 100-yard repeats. Take about eight yoga breaths between repeats. Your sole focus on these repeats is to develop your instinct for fluent, relaxed, and controlled swimming. Using SSPs will help you develop focus — and prepare you for the race itself. Change your SSP after every one or two 100s (see pages 136-137 for SSP ideas). Practice will tell you if one or another SSP makes a noticeable difference in your stroke. If so, on race day you can focus on that feeling. If you lose the feeling of ease, take a longer rest (more yoga breaths) and/or slow down.

3. Build distance, but maintain efficiency/economy. Next step is to start increasing your benchmark set, but to keep the focus on doing it as easily as possible. Do each set twice a week, following a prolonged warmup of drills and/or swimming with fistgloves®. Modify weekly according to the instructions to allow you to build toward the Ironman distance. Modify only one variable each week. All other variables remain as before.

Week 1. Swim 15 x 100. Keep using yoga breaths (6 to 8) as your interval. Choose a new SSP focal point after every one or two 100s. Maintain average stroke count at least 10% lower than on your initial test swim. (I.e., if you averaged 20 spl, aim for 18 on your 100s). Never breathe hard. Finish the set feeling as if you could easily keep going that way for another five or more 100s. (NOTE: If at any time your stroke count or sense of control starts to deteriorate, pause the set and do a recovery 50 of your favorite stroke drill.)

Week 2. Decrease rest by 1 breath.

Week 3. Pick up the pace slightly over the last 3 to 4 x 100.

Week 4. Decrease average spl by 1.

Week 5. Increase # of repeats to 20 x 100.

Week 6. Decrease rest by 1 breath.

Week 7. Pick up the pace slightly over the last 6 to 8 x 100.

Week 8. Increase # of repeats to 25 x 100.

Week 9. Decrease rest by 1 breath.

Week 10. Increase # of repeats to 30 x 100.

Week 11. Increase # of repeats to 35 x 100.

Week 12. Increase # of repeats to 40 x 100.

Don't view these guidelines as an all-or-nothing proposition. You don't fail the course if you can't stay precisely with the weekly schedule. They're intended more as a suggested model for a smart, systematic, progressive approach to set design by establishing a pattern of *effective* swimming — efficient stroke, consistent pace, low energy cost, moderate recovery between repeats — and train yourself to maintain that effective swimming pattern over progressively greater distances. This training format will do far more to reinforce the qualities that produce the BEST long-distance swim, the ability to swim economically at a target pace for a long time.

Add Variety to Your Distance Training with "Smart Sets"

To add variety to your training program, you could do a weekly practice composed of multiple rounds of "smart sets," such as the set of 5 X 100 described on page 163. This offers you almost limitless options for how to train. Here is a sample long set of 4000 yards — just short of Ironman distance — presented in numerous ways to show the rich range of possibilities. You could adjust this set to rounds of 3 X 100 or 4 X 100 if you are training for "shorter" distances than an Ironman.

Swim 8 rounds of 5 x 100

1st Option: Keep stroke count the same, but descend your time on each repeat in a round. (You'll be descending 8 times.)

2nd Option: Alternate 5 x 100 Silent Swimming with 5 x 100 in which you add one stroke to each successive repeat and descend your time, until 8 rounds are complete.

3rd Option: Swim one round keeping your time the same but subtracting one stroke from each successive repeat, then swim one round keeping your time and stroke count the same on each repeat, then swim one round holding the same stroke count but descending your time on each repeat, then swim one round adding one stroke to each repeat and descending your time. Then repeat rounds one through four.

4th Option: Alternate one round of keeping your time the same but subtracting one stroke from each repeat, with one round of adding one stroke to each repeat and descending your time, until 8 rounds are complete.

By using the set-design options to make each round slightly different from the others, you'll have created a far more interesting and valuable way to "get in your long swims."

Swimming longer sets in rounds with regular shifts in focus — or setting up a particular pattern and repeating it — is far better than a straight, unvarying set of 25 or 30 x 100. Such cycle training heightens your focus, making excellence more consistent in your swimming. Each round becomes a learning experience that prepares you to raise your performance in the next round and the next, until late in the set, when you'd normally be struggling to hold on — both physically and mentally — you're feeling in control and at your best. This is the ideal preparation for swims longer than 1-kilometer.

How many rounds should you do? You'll obviously be conscious of how far you need to swim during the race but you should be even more conscious of your limitations as a developing swimmer: Work patiently toward sets of that distance, adding repeats or rounds — or increasing repeat distance — only as you develop your ability to swim that far with ease and control and an SL of your choice. Practicing struggle in order to "go the distance" won't benefit you in any way. But your stroke count will always give you "early warning" of when you should modify or cut short a planned set or workout.

What to do when your stroke count goes up? You don't necessarily have to end the set immediately. You could give yourself a bit more rest between repeats. You could add a bit of recovery with an extra 100 of your favorite drill or SSP between rounds of 5 x 100. You could continue using the SSP during the 100s: Try to pierce the water better, make sure water is flowing over the back or your head, or swim a bit more quietly, for instance. Often, that's all it takes to sustain your SL and repeat times as fatigue begins to mount. And as soon as you acquire the presence of mind to make these kinds of strategic choices, you've added one more tool to your racing skill set.

Should I Ever Do a Long Swim?

What's the place of the marathon swim? Do a longer swim (1000 to 2000 yards) once or twice a month to check your ability to hold a lower spl with greater ease for progressively longer distances than your initial test. You will see much greater and much more reliable progress than if you were on a steady diet of long swims or generic repeats.

Should I Ever Swim Anything Except Freestyle?

Nearly half of those who swim with the Masters in New Paltz are triathletes, with the multi-sporters themselves divided into two further groups: About half cheerfully (or dutifully) do whatever the coach assigns, even a set of 100-IMs (individual medley) swims or 50-breast-kick reps. The rest are reluctant to do anything but freestyle, concluding, with what seems inarguable logic, that the best use of their time is to focus on the stroke they'll use in races.

As an open-water racer, my swimming needs and goals are similar to those of triathletes. And yet I swim other strokes at least 30% of the time in my training, and work tirelessly on improving my technique and efficiency in *all* of them. Why? Because I've learned that multi-dimensional training makes me a better freestyler.

I have also coached elite-level swimmers, both sprint and distance freestylers, with the same mix of 30 to 40 percent other strokes and 60 to 70 percent freestyle. At times they did less than 40 percent of their training in freestyle. Why? Because experience has proven to me that, without exception, their freestyle improved more with varied training than when they trained only in freestyle.

The most important reason is that too much of anything usually leads to staleness in that activity. I swim stronger, smoother, and faster freestyle when I swim it more sparingly. The other strokes keep my "freestyle muscles" fresher, by giving them a form of active rest, helping me maintain a higher level of effort and efficiency on every freestyle lap I do.

Second, training with all four strokes produces more training adaptations. As I explained in Chapter 15, once the body acclimates to any type of training, the opportunity for further adaptation decreases. The more one-dimensional a training program, the more quickly the body adapts, limiting your potential for improvement. Employing more modes of training gives you more opportunities to get your body thinking: "This is a new task; I'd better attack it with all the vigor I have available." One workshop alum (a triathlete and recent convert to four-stroke training) told us in a recent e-mail: "I finally realized that when I swim just freestyle, my body experiences a limited range of effort and fatigue. It's kind of like running or biking the same loop every day — you know every dip and hill, and have cracked their codes so well that your body runs on auto-pilot. Swimming a different stroke is like tackling a brand new course. My body learns to deal with unexpected demands — just as it will have to do when I race on an unfamiliar course or under unpredictable conditions. The physical and mental benefits have been powerful."

Third, a key ingredient of a quality workout is using as much of the body's muscle tissue as possible. Freestyle workouts use the same muscle groups over and over. Training in a medley of strokes (or drills) recruits the largest number of muscle groups possible. Such workouts are also less likely to cause overuse injuries. By spreading the workload over more joints and movement patterns, you reduce the potential for repetitive overwork in any particular motion.

Fourth, my motivation and enjoyment are greater when I vary my training. With a variety of strokes and drills, I can set an endless range of personal goals, and devise an endless number of interesting, challenging workouts to achieve them. I get as much of a charge from a personal-best breaststroke swimming-golf score as I do from improving my freestyle golf score. And since my potential in the other strokes remains relatively less tapped than in free, personal training achievements happen with greater frequency, keeping me fresher both mentally and physically.

For all these reasons, I never "go through the motions" on the other strokes, just because they're not freestyle. I try to swim them with the same high expectations as in freestyle. The better the quality of my interaction with the water in *any* form, the more I learn about aquatic fluency and economy in general. Working on this puzzle in so many varied ways keeps my learning curve steep and my interest high.

In some cases, the crossover learning is quite direct. Swimming or drilling in backstroke provide different insights about body balance, alignment, and rotation than those I learn when doing freestyle, but the learning translates *directly* to my freestyle. The other strokes make my freestyle better in less direct, but still valuable ways. Simply by increasing the variety of my interactions with the water, my body becomes a better instrument for moving through water. And when that happens, my freestyle improves. I'd guess I've stretched my horizon for continued freestyle improvement by a good ten years, simply by training in such a multi-dimensional way.

Best of all, to gain such benefits yourself doesn't mean you need to swim an advanced or race-legal butterfly or breaststroke. You can learn precisely the lessons you are ready to absorb by practicing fluent, coordinated movement in whatever way you're able. Backstroke drills can teach you lessons just as valuable as backstroke swimming. Short-axis drills may teach you even more than swimming whole-stroke in fly or breast because the full strokes require more advanced skills. Fly and breast drills can be quite simple and easy to learn, and you'll benefit more by practicing smooth, fluent, and *effortless* "butterfly-like-movement" in a drill than by swimming butterstruggle.

You can teach yourself an entire range of "different strokes" skills with the aid of two TI videos: *Freestyle and Backstroke: the Total Immersion Way* and *Butterfly and Breaststroke: the Total Immersion Way*. Here's a quick set of efficient-swimming tips for when you do try those other strokes:

Fishlike Backstroke

As in free, swim backstroke mainly on your side. Your power is limited when you swim "upside down and backwards," so it's even more important to be "slippery."

Body/Head Position
- *Hide your head*, keeping it completely still and your chin slightly tucked.
- Lean on your upper back as you roll from side to side.

Legs
- Kick compactly with a long, supple leg, with no knee bend and with your feet toed in slightly.
- Your kick rotates as your body rolls; the beat is generally more steady than in freestyle.

Arms
- Stretch your bodyline as your hand slices cleanly and deeply (pinkie first) into the water.
- Keep arms exactly opposite each other and linked to body-roll rhythms.
- Fistgloves® can be even more valuable in backstroke than in freestyle.

Fishlike Butterfly

Never practice "butterstruggle." Don't fight gravity; *hug the surface* at all times. Keep your head in a neutral position during and after breathing.

Body/Head Position
- Swim as close to the surface — both above and below — as possible; channel your energy forward, not up and down.
- Keep your head as close as possible to a neutral position at all times; use a "sneaky breath."
- Keep legs relaxed and let them follow core-body undulation.

Arms
- Land *forward*; don't crash or dive down after recovery.
- To stroke, sweep your hands in toward your chin, then immediately flare them out to a "karate-chop" exit.
- Recover with a relaxed, sweeping motion.

Breathing
- Breathe early in the pull, without raising or jutting your chin.
- Look down slightly ("sneaky" breath).

Fishlike Breaststroke

The keys to efficiency are to streamline your entire body as you finish each stroke and to keep your head in a neutral position at *all* times.

Body/Head Position
- Look down slightly as you breathe, and keep your head in line with your spine — as if wearing a neck brace.
- Stretch and streamline your body fully at the end of each stroke.

Legs
- "Sneak" the legs up, inside the "hole" your body travels through.
- "Grab" water at top of kick, then push it back with feet wider than hips
- Finish by pointing your toes, and *squeezing* the water from between your feet and legs.

Arms

- Keep pull compact and quick; better too small than too big.
- Always keep hands where you can see them — as far forward as possible during entire pull.
- After outsweep, spin your hands directly back to meet far in front of your face.

Timing

- Initiate recovery by *kicking your hands forward.*
- Your hands should reach full extension as your face lays back on the water.
- Change your rhythm in the core, not in your arms and legs. Rock your chest and hips slowly when swimming slowly. Rock them faster to swim faster.

Sample All-Stroke Training Session

Warmup

400 Mixed Strokes (25FR+25BK+25BR...)
4 x 50 short-axis pulsing with fins
(25 Head Lead — 25 Hand Lead)

Swimming Golf Set (all with fistgloves®)

Descend golf score on each round.
4 x 50 BK
4 x 50 (25BK+25FR)
4 x 50 FR

Stroke-Counting Set

5 x 100, maintaining same total stroke count on all five 100s
1st 100: BK
2nd 100: 75BK+25FR
3rd 100: 50BK+50FR
4th 100: 25BK+75FR
5th 100: 100 FR

Main Set

    4 rounds of 3 x 100

    1st 100 of each Round: BK   Slide & Glide drill

    2nd 100 of each Round: IM   Silent and count strokes

    3rd 100 of each Round: FR   Brisk and count strokes

    Use 100 BK and 100 IM as active recovery, allowing stronger, faster swims on the four repeats of 100 FR.

Cooldown

    6 x 50 Long-Axis Combo (1st 25: 4BK/3FR, 2nd 25: 3BK/4FR)

Total Yardage: 3200

    The drills mentioned in this practice and throughout this book are described and illustrated in the videos *Freestyle and Backstroke: The TI Way* and *Butterfly and Breaststroke: The TI Way*. For more sample training sets, visit www.totalimmersion.net.

* * *

    There you have it, all the forms of training you could possibly need to do. But you're wondering when we'll tell you how to use your buoys and paddles. Well, turn to Chapter 18 to find out.

Pool Tools: Less Is More

A s I mention adding "tools" to your skill set, you may be wondering where does all that seemingly essential stuff — kickboards, pull buoys, and hand paddles — fit in the Total Immersion program? They don't, actually, except in specialized cases. It's true that virtually everyone uses them, but this is one of those cases where most folks just have the wrong idea about what these training aids really do. So let's take a critical look at training tools.

Of all the elements that make up the inexact gift known as "swimming talent," the most considerable is extraordinary kinesthetic awareness — gifted swimmers just know how to work *with* the water better than anyone else to achieve less resistance and fluid movement. But, as I've tried to make clear, a surprising amount of what coaches call "talent" is *learnable*. "Average" swimmers can unquestionably heighten their own kinesthetic awareness (with drills, SSPs, stroke counting, fistgloves®, etc.) and doing so will always produce more improvement, more quickly, than anything under the heading of "work." Most training tools have two drawbacks: (1) they encourage you to focus on effort, rather than efficiency; or (2) they actively interfere with your ability to improve your kinesthetic awareness. Finally, for developing swimmers and triathletes (athletes who have a large set of skills to acquire and a limited amount of pool time to do so), there is also the issue of prioritizing precious time for activities that have the largest value. TI methods help you swim better *immediately.* Buoys, boards, and paddles simply don't.

Just Say No to Kickboards

Let's cover the shortcomings of each, starting with kickboards. Earlier, I wrote that the ideal kick for a triathlete, or anyone swimming longer distances, is one that is non-overt and nearly effortless. But the main idea of kickboard training is to get your legs in shape for working *harder.* And they don't even do that. The flutter used on a kickboard — with arms, torso and hips rigidly locked in place — is so different from the kick swimmers use when swimming that kickboard sets have zero value for developing a synergistic, non-overt kick. Ditto for "conditioning your legs."

Because your legs move so differently when kicking on a board than while swimming, the only thing a kickboard really trains you for is pushing a kickboard. If someone held a bizarre triathlon that required the swim leg to be done on a kickboard, then training with one would make sense; otherwise, *it's a total waste of time!* If you want your legs to be "in shape" for swimming, the relaxed kicking you do while practicing TI drills conditions your legs to do exactly what they need to do when you race: stay relaxed. You are dispensed from using a kickboard ever again.

Lose the Buoy

Pull buoys have one central drawback: They fool you into thinking you've solved balance. They're so popular with triathletes — and thousands of other swimmers — because poor balance is such a common problem. So long as you have a buoy on, it supports your hips and legs. You feel better and swim faster. Naturally you want to use it more and more. The problem is that using it never seems to teach you how to stay balanced *after* you take the buoy off. As soon as you remove the buoy, that sinking feeling is right back and you're no better off than you were before. Want to feel better *without* the buoy — permanently? Balance drills, SSPs such as Hiding Your Head and Swimming Downhill, and swimming with fistgloves® produce lasting lessons in how to stay balanced while you swim.

And forget the idea that training with a buoy strengthens your pull by overloading and isolating your arms. In fact, if anything, it does just the opposite. Because the artificial buoyancy of the buoy raises your body in the water, it *underloads* your arms — no training benefit at all. That would be bad enough, but using a buoy can actually hurt your stroking power. That's because power doesn't come from the arms; it comes from core-body rotation. Buoys can easily inhibit your body roll, interfering with your rhythm and power. Fortunately, once you do learn balance, putting on a buoy should feel all wrong, which will soon discourage you from using one.

The sole circumstance in which there might be some value in using a buoy is this: If you are one of those extremely lean and/or densely muscled athletes who seems permanently balance-challenged...if you experience what feels like terminal struggle while doing balance drills...if you have a "frantic" kick...you may be able to selectively use a buoy as an alternate way to learn balance. Using a fairly small, light buoy, swim a relaxed 25. Keep your head hidden and swim as silently as you can. As you do, tune in to how it feels to be supported, to be able to float an unhurried arm forward and swim a little "taller," to be able to *let go of your kick*. Can't feel it after one length? Do a few more 25s that way. When those sensations come, just capture and imprint them. Then remove the buoy and swim 2 x 25s without it. Hide your head and swim downhill. Swim as gently and quietly as possible. You have just one goal: to get your no-buoy laps to feel as much like the buoy lap as possible. Patiently repeat this pattern for 10 or 15 minutes. As your no-buoy laps begin to feel as relaxed as the buoyed laps, add more unbuoyed 25s.

Smart Hands Are Better than Dumb Plastic

The rap on hand paddles is pretty simple. You put them on and suddenly feel as if you can really grab and hold the water and move it where you want to. If only they'd let you wear them while racing. But...they don't, so at some point you have to figure out how to feel that way without them. Unfortunately, after you do take them off, you feel like you're trying to row with popsicle sticks. What could be good about that?

Now consider what happens when you wear fistgloves®. You feel, at first, as if you can't do *anything* with the water, but you gradually regain a good deal of your control. Then, when you take them off, your own hands suddenly feel like *dinner plates* and they magically know how to work *with* the water. So which tool produces the more desirable learning effect? I rest my case.

As with pull buoys, however, there is one small exception. Paddles are usually emphasized as a power tool (and the bigger the paddle, the better — or so the theory goes). You use the extra surface area to muscle the water. Unless you have a *perfect* stroke, muscling the water with paddles is mainly a good way to improve your chances of shoulder injury. Instead, you might occasionally don small paddles for a few superslow laps with a narrow focus on how they may help your hand learn to *pierce* the water...or slide weightlessly forward a looong way...or anchor for the catch. Then remove them and, as suggested above for buoy use, try to recreate that sensation without the paddles. Unless you can subtract at least two strokes with the paddles on, they're not helping you at all.

Fins as a Learning Aid, Not for Temporary Speed

The most common use of fins among triathletes, it seems, is by those who have been stuck in the 1:40 lane on 100-yard repeats at Masters practice and just know they'd swim much better if they could only join the party in the 1:30 lane. So they put on Zoomers and instantly can swim much faster repeats. But those race directors stubbornly refuse to let you wear them when it counts. And, as with buoys and paddles, that's just the problem with the way most people use fins. They are a temporary and artificial aid that helps you swim easier or faster while you have them on — but the effect disappears as soon as you take them off. No learning happens. *None.* Wearing fins to be faster is like wearing platform shoes to be taller.

What fins might do, when used this way, is interfere with your ability to develop a fluent, relaxed, efficient stroke into a reliable habit. Cut-off fins, in particular, are *specifically* designed to help you kick faster than you could with full-blade fins. And the faster your legs move, the faster your arms have to move to keep up. Isn't faster turnover (i.e., higher SR) precisely what we're trying to *avoid*? Short fins were designed originally to help sprint swimmers achieve high stroke rates while swimming with fin-aided speed — and to condition a swimmer's legs for the *hard* kicking that is typical when sprinting. Again, that's precisely the kind of thing a smart triathlete wants to avoid.

There are exceptions with fins as well. I've already described the ways in which they can be useful as an aid to mastering drills, if you have a non-propulsive kick. And they can also be useful in helping you expand your range of swimming skills, by working on Short Axis skills from the video *Butterfly and Breaststroke: The Total Immersion Way*.

So, besides helping you avoid wasted time and energy by using useless tools, we've also helped you lighten your swim bag considerably.

Taking Care of Your Body

T his book is not intended to be the last word on all aspects of
swimming, so I won't attempt exhaustive detail on what coaches
call "dryland training." But as a relatively new swimmer, you
deserve at least a "quick-start guide" of the sort that comes with a new com-
puter. The essentials include "prehab" exercises to keep your shoulders
healthy and pain-free, plus basic guidance on sensible strength training that
will help your body perform optimally. Let's begin with shoulder exercises.

Preventing Shoulder Injury: A Quick and Simple Plan

Swimming deserves its reputation for being both vigorous and gentle. But "gentle" doesn't guarantee "injury-free," particularly when it
comes to your shoulder, which is almost ideally built for trouble.
Shoulder anatomy looks like a racquetball (the head of your upper arm
bone) balanced on a bottle cap (the socket of the scapula.) The ball is
held on the bottle cap by a network of 17 muscles. This is great for mobil-
ity, but terrible for accelerating your arm rearwards against resistance.
"Swimmer's shoulder" is common among swimmers because "human
swimmers" instinctively try to muscle the water — rather than anchor the
hand and let the kinetic chain do the work. The resulting over-stretched
rotator-cuff muscles allow the arm bone (a.k.a. the humerus) to wobble
in its socket. This pinches the muscles and tendons that stabilize your
shoulder, causing inflammation and pain.

Because a swimmer's shoulder rotates 1,200 to 1,500 times every mile, a prevention plan is clearly in order. The most important muscles to strengthen are the rotator cuff muscles, which anchor and stabilize the head of the humerus, allowing the other shoulder muscles to perform effectively, and the scapular (shoulder blade) stabilizers, which protect against pinched tendons and rotator cuff stress. The primary virtue of this routine is that it requires little time (10 minutes, three times per week) and little equipment. All you need for those exercises specifying the use of resistance is StrechCordz™ (see resource section for order info), a thera-band, or light weights — keep it light enough to do at least 10 to 15 repetitions of each exercise. Work until you feel fatigue; rest and do a second set, for at least 20 to 30 reps of each. Try to build to 30 or more repetitions in a single set (no second set necessary when you do) before fatigue.

Strengthen Your Rotator Cuff Muscles

Exercise #1. Stand with arms at your sides, a dumbbell in each hand. Roll your shoulders forward, up toward your ears, back, then down again, moving through the greatest possible range of movement. Alternate one front-to-back rotation, with one in the opposite direction.

Exercise #2. Lie on your side with your head propped on your hand and your top arm against your side, bent at a right angle with knuckles forward and palm down, holding a light weight. Keep the upper arm against your body as you slowly rotate your forearm until your knuckles point to the sky then return at the same speed.

You can also do this exercise while standing, with StrechCordz™ or a theraband for resistance. Hold your arms close to your body in a "shake-hands" position with your elbows held into your ribs. (Place a thin cushion or pillow between elbow and ribs for greater stability.) Grasp the ends of the StrechCordz™ or theraband in your hands. Rotate your forearms slowly out to the side, then return at the same speed.

Exercise #3. Sit or stand with your arms straight and hanging at your side. Leading with your thumb, slowly raise your arms to just below and just in front of your shoulder, pause for a moment, then return at the same speed. Use a light weight of 5 to 8 pounds, a theraband or StrechCordz™ for resistance.

Exercise #4. Bend at the waist, with your arms hanging straight from your shoulders. (Soften your knees to avoid lower-back strain.) Leading with your knuckles and slightly-bent elbows, raise your arms slowly to shoulder level, pause for a moment, then return at the same speed.

Strengthen Your Scapular Stabilizers

Exercise #1. Sit on a firm surface with your feet flat on the floor. Place your hands on seat or arm rests. Straighten your elbows and push down, lifting your hips off the chair. (If necessary, help by pushing a bit with your feet; as you get stronger let your arms do more of the work.) You can do this one at work! At the pool, do this on a stack of kickboards.

Exercise #2. Place your hands on a stable surface (a starting block at the pool, counter, desk, the back of a couch, almost anything that's 3 to 4 feet high). Position your feet so that you are in a semi-standing "push-up" position with hands at shoulder width and arms straight. Do a slow pushup — *but without bending your elbows.* Keep your arms straight, and lower your chest a few inches as your shoulder blades pinch together. Then, using shoulder muscles, press back up, rounding your shoulders and spreading your shoulder blades as much as possible. As you grow stronger, move toward a more horizontal position, eventually doing it in a pushup or "plank" position.

Exercise #3. Attach a theraband or StrechCordz™ to a stable object at waist or chest height. Grasp the ends and with your arms straight in front and your shoulders down away from your ears, pull your shoulders back (pinching shoulder blades together) then return them forward at the same speed, until you feel your shoulder blades stretch wide. Move slowly enough to feel the muscles in the middle of your back contract and relax.

Exercise #4. Lie on your stomach, with a rolled towel under your forehead and a pillow under your hips. Extend your arms forward from your shoulders (biceps two inches from your ears), elbows straight and thumbs up. Raise your arms as far as possible, without bending your elbows; hold them at their highest point for a moment, then lower slowly. Feel the effort from your shoulders to the middle of your back. Start with no weight; work up to 2 to 5 pounds. This and the next exercise can also be done on a swiss ball.

Exercise #5. Lie on your stomach, with a rolled towel under your forehead and a pillow under your hips. Extend your arms to the sides at shoulder level with palms down or forward, (thumbs pointing up). Keeping elbows straight, pinch your shoulder blades together as you lift your arms; pause at the highest point for a moment, then lower slowly. Do this with or without light weights.

Stretch the Muscles Under the Shoulder

Swimming promotes natural flexibility and fights the stiffness of aging better than any other sport, but it's not enough by itself. If you do no others, at least use the stretches described below. They will target the muscles you use most. Do one or both of each pair of exercises, holding each stretch for 10 or more yoga breaths, before and particularly after swimming.

Stretch #1. Raise one arm above your head, dropping your hand behind your shoulder. Lean the back of your elbow against a corner of a wall and press until you feel a stretch from the elbow down to your armpit and below.

Stretch #2. Put both arms overhead in the streamlined position. Lean first to the left side as far as possible, then to the right. Feel the pull all the way down your side.

Stretch the Muscles in Front of the Shoulder

Stretch #1. Hold one arm out to your side at a right angle; bend your elbow 90 degrees with fingers up and palm forward. Brace the inside surface of your hand-forearm-elbow against the corner of a wall with your elbow at shoulder height. Press against the wall, turning your opposite hip back until you feel a stretch across the front of your shoulder and upper chest.

Stretch #2. Repeat with your elbow braced at ear level.

Stretch the Muscles in Back of the Shoulder

Stretch #1. Place the back of your hand on your lower back with your elbow out to the side. Brace the inside of your elbow against the corner of a wall, while turning your opposite hip forward until you feel a stretch across the back of your shoulder.

Stretch #2. Put one arm across your body so that the shoulder is under your chin and your hand, forearm, and upper arm parallel to the ground. Without turning your body, use your other hand to pull the arm as close to your chest as possible.

Strength Training the Total Immersion Way

Many swimmers are tempted to think they can overpower the water by bulking up. But water, being a fluid medium, just doesn't respond to sheer power. The water's resistance will always surpass any strength you can apply and, besides, it takes a special kind of strength, accurately applied, to overcome the water's resistance.

The strength you build with, say, intensive bench presses is best at helping you do more intensive bench presses. The world's best swimmers don't have bulky or highly defined muscles. The strength that produces world records, as well helping anyone to swim efficiently, fluently, and enjoyably is more like that exhibited by the slim, graceful cables that hold up the Brooklyn Bridge than by the brutes who heft enormous poundage in weightlifting competitions. (Which is not to say that conventional weightlifting has no value for swimmers; if you do go to a gym, ask a trainer to help plan a program of compound/complex exercises for general strength development)

But what may be even more valuable is "functional strength," the kind that makes us more robust in everything from spading the garden to shoveling the walk to swimming 1500 meters. And that means training muscles and joints to work as they do when we move — multiple muscle groups, multiple joints, and complex planes of movement, all at once. This is because fast swimming isn't produced by muscling your way through the water, but by maintaining body positions that minimize drag and connect the propelling armstrokes to the power of the core-body's "kinetic chain." That kind of strength is developed by practicing challenging movements that teach torso and arm/shoulder muscles to work together.

My yoga practice feels utterly functional for swimming because it teaches me to use my body as a system, working all muscle groups in unison, against the resistance of gravity and my own inflexibility to build strength and flexibility with each movement. Exercises such as pushups, pull-ups, dips, step-ups, and squats, done with just the weight of your own body, also develop muscle sense and joint stability, letting tendons and ligaments adapt rather than being overwhelmed as they sometimes are by machines or external weight.

Especially critical to functional strength is "core strength," which means strength in the abdominal muscles, spinal rotators and erectors, hip flexors, the glutes, and more. If your core isn't strong, then neither are you because your torso is the force coupler, which transmits power from legs to upper body. Abdominal exercises of all sorts, and particularly Pilates exercises develop core power. I take Pilates classes with a certified instructor and practice on my own with the aid of a book (see Resources for more information on yoga and Pilates.)

On the Ball

One of the best developers of functional and core strength is Swiss Ball exercise. Here's my favorite series

To Begin. Balance in a horizontal position with the ball below your hips, hands directly under your shoulders, and legs straight behind, parallel to the floor.

Action: Walk your hands out until the ball is at your knees. Pause for two slow breaths, then walk back. Repeat 10 times.

Key Point: Maintain a straight, horizontal line from your shoulders to your feet.

"Advanced Placement": Try any of the following:

1. While pausing with the ball under your knees, rock your chest down toward the floor – your legs and feet will rise and the line from hands to feet will get straighter.

2. Walk out until the ball is under your shins or ankles, then walk it back to your hips. Don't let your back sway or bend; keep your hips in line with your spine and feet.

3. With the ball under your knees, roll it under your left knee, then under your right.

In each of these exercises you'll feel yourself contracting a connected band of muscle from your hands to your hips – exactly the way you should feel your strength while swimming. The variations will each recruit different stabilizer muscles into the action. This training is as swimming-functional as anything you can do on land.

Dear Terry,

Success! On May 27, 2001, I completed the Keauhou-Kona Half Ironman. I was ecstatic, not just because it was my first Half Ironman but because I stayed in control during the 1.2-mile swim. Since I began doing triathlons, I routinely panic during the swim. It's easy doing lap after lap in a pool, but the same distance when measured out in X number of buoys in a lake or the ocean has always been an intimidating sight. I hyperventilate as soon as we're in the water, I'm afraid of being left behind. Everything falls apart when I try to chase the other swimmers and subsequently flail and struggle my way to shore. After repeated experiences like this, I doubted everything: my training, my body, and my mental state. Thoughts of not starting the race, thoughts of drowning, flailing, struggling, and, finally, the humiliation of an inevitable rescue crossed my mind countless times. But stubborn as I am, I refused to give up without a fight.

Prior to this race, I swam daily to get used to the water — the taste, sights, and swells. I repeatedly visualized the swim start and the entire swim itself, seeing myself going out with the rest of the athletes, one stroke at a time, breathe in, breathe out, sighting the big orange buoys, the King Kam Hotel, and finish. Every night when I went to bed, I filled my head with encouraging thoughts of swimming smoothly.

When race morning finally arrived, I was calm and determined. I positioned myself at the back left of the crowd. When the air horn went off, I dived in with the others, focusing on one stroke at a time. I started slow, stayed calm, and found my "groove." Five minutes into the swim, I realized I was completely comfortable and immediately became more relaxed; the rest of the swim was a breeze. I wore a big smile all the way from the turnaround buoy to the swim finish. It felt so easy I even wished I could swim some more, but it was time to get on the bike. I knew I couldn't possibly have a bad race because I'd just had the most magical swim in my entire life.

Thanks for this experience,

Jo Wang

The lesson: It's reasonable, even logical, to feel intimidated by open-water racing. But it's not inevitable. By rehearsing with a plan and then simply following your plan during the race, you'll learn to LOVE the swimming part of any triathlon, no matter the distance.

Part 5

Getting Ready to Race

We've come a long way together and I hope you've enjoyed the experience. You've learned how to turn frustration into fulfillment, how to teach yourself a new stroke, and how to systematically expand your mastery by practicing at a variety of speeds and SL/SR combinations. Now it's time to put those lessons to the test. Because I'm a swimming (not multisport) coach, I won't presume to advise you how to race once you leave the water. But having raced in open water since 1972, I'll share what I've learned about how to make every race satisfying and pleasurable. The first lesson is to rehearse prior to the race and then to swim the race as you've rehearsed. We've already covered neoprene-free swimming in exhaustive detail, so now let's shift our focus to how to use your wetsuit in the smartest way possible.

Dress Rehearsal

I have only 10 minutes of wetsuit experience, but after swimming with a group of triathletes — most of them novice swimmers — during a TI triathlon camp in late August of 2000, I learned priceless lessons about how rehearsal and a wetsuit *strategy* can put any triathlete in the driver's seat. Although you will assuredly swim faster with a wetsuit, that will not be the most important factor. The ease and control you can gain will be far more critical to your overall race experience.

We began the camp, in Killington, Vermont, with several days devoted to mastering the drills presented in the Lessons section, and had done little whole-stroke swimming before we went to Chittenden Reservoir to test those pool lessons. At the reservoir, the coaches swam without wetsuits; the campers — several of whom had never swum outside the "friendly confines" of a pool before — were neoprene-clad. Our first reservoir session was limited to brief distances (60 to 100 strokes) simply to acclimate to swimming without lanes and walls — and to the disorientation and general unease that often comes with that. For the first 30 minutes, we practiced a variety of SSPs, mainly to get everyone so focused on technique that they wouldn't pause to think: "Where's the wall?" Then we spent another 30 minutes learning basic navigation skills: how to sight without interrupting your rhythm and flow and how to closely follow other swimmers. We swam slowly so everyone could maintain comfortable proximity over the short distances we traversed.

Two days later, we returned for a final open-water rehearsal before the Vermont State Triathlon Championships, which would be the "final exam" for our 6-day camp. Our plan was to swim a triangular course of about 1200 meters. The first leg was roughly 300 meters to a well-marked rocky point on the reservoir's eastern shore. Then, after reconnoitering, 600 meters to a boathouse on the west shore, before returning the final 300 meters to the boat ramp from which we started.

On the first leg, two or three faster swimmers (those with competitive swimming experience) took off at a brisk pace. Immediately, most of the 20-odd other campers, anxious not to get left behind, took up the chase. And just as quickly, all the week's hard-won lessons in efficiency were forgotten, as most degenerated into churning. There were many discouraged looks and heaving chests at our first checkpoint. Before beginning the long east-west leg, I reminded everyone of our mantra: "Never practice struggle." My instructions were to swim as slowly as necessary to cultivate a sense of comfort and control. "Just start at a leisurely pace — like a warmup — and find a rhythm that you can maintain indefinitely. Keep the group in sight, *but don't try to keep up*. Do whatever it takes to stay relaxed and in control. Focus on one SSP if it helps. If you feel yourself getting rough, *slow down*, until you 'find your groove' again."

Immediately, the difference in "group flow" was marked. From my vantage point bringing up the rear, it was evident that splashing and flailing had been transformed into smooth, controlled movement. And the group did a much better job of staying together, despite the increased swimming distance. When we gathered again, satisfied smiles had replaced long faces. "That actually felt good," someone said.

After a brief stop, we began the final 300-meter leg. When everyone had finished, there was palpable *elation* over what they had done and how they felt. Several stood on the boat ramp surveying the course and shaking their heads. "I can't believe we just swam that far. Not only that, I could go back out right now and do it again." Which is just what several did, wading back in to do another quarter mile, one saying, "That felt so good, I just want to keep swimming."

Back at the lodge that night, we reviewed the lessons learned:

1. No matter how much you may have practiced efficiency in the pool, once the horn sounds, it's easy to lose your wits. All your instincts — not just competitive, but *survival* — are warning you not to fall back, lest you find yourself *alone* out there. Chasing the leaders (or anyone in front of you) is your main thought.

2. Unless you have a *lot* of experience in swimming races (and I mean at a fairly high level), and particularly in open -water racing, chasing quickly degenerates into churning, which brings rapid exhaustion, anxiety, loss of any sense of control, and *no material gain in speed.*

3. If you just stop chasing and find your own best, sustained, pace, you swim a lot better with a lot less effort.

Tortoises Swim Better than Hares

You wouldn't try to run with a world-class runner, or cycle with a world-class biker. This is even truer in the water, not just in how fast you may swim, but particularly in how *hard.* Your swimming experience dictates your race plan, and there are only a couple dozen athletes in the entire triathlon universe who have enough swimming experience to swim hard and not blow the whole race. Swimmers such as Joanna Zeiger and Sheila Taormina had *millions* of yards — in training and racing — to learn to tolerate high heart rates and stroke rates without blowing up before they ever raced a triathlon. But *every* triathlete can learn, right now, how to use a wetsuit intelligently to gain control and save critical energy. Toward that end, here's how you can turn a wetsuit to your advantage.

- First, a wetsuit takes away the feeling that you have to keep your arms turning over just to keep from sinking. Take advantage of that by relaxing, and enjoy the wonderful and rare security of feeling completely supported by the water.
- Once you feel supported, it becomes much easier to use your arms to lengthen your bodyline. Glide your hand forward — almost as if stretching for something just out of reach — before anchoring your hand for the pull. This will keep your stroke tempo feeling almost leisurely.

- Particularly in the first 100 to 200 meters, stay *well* within yourself. Go even slower than you think necessary until nervousness dissipates and you feel calm and in control. Use that control to focus on one or two of your favorite SSPs.
- Once you "find your groove," don't be tempted to go faster if you think it feels too easy. Just float along behind someone moving at what feels like a pace you could sustain indefinitely. At the end of the day, you'll gain far more time if you just keep your heart rate down, than if you try to catch or stay with faster swimmers. I promise you'll find yourself passing dozens of competitors on the bike or run if you swim more economically than they do. In fact, you'll probably pass quite a few of them during the latter stages of the swim — without even trying — simply because as you just keep moving at your relaxed, steady pace, the hares will come back to you.

Focal Points for Wetsuit Wearers

1. Because balance will become a "no-brainer," you won't have to focus on *swimming downhill*. Your hips and legs should be light and riding high.

2. Even though you won't pay as heavy a penalty for it, you should still avoid a high head position. Your movements will be smoother and more fluent because your body likes head-spine alignment and is designed to work best that way. So keep looking down as you swim — except when getting your bearings.

3. Keep focused on lengthening your body with each stroke. Let the pull part of the stroke happen on its own, while you attentively slide each hand into the water and extend it, like putting your arm into a sleeve. Once your stroking hand passes your head, shift your attention to the one extending forward.

4. Set and change your stroke tempo in the core. Maintain a comfortable pace with a relaxed body-rolling tempo. If you want to go a little faster, do it by moving your belly-button faster, not your arms and legs.

5. Avoid over-swimming and loss of control by making sure you feel your hands are moving at the same speed as your body. Swim with your whole body as a unit, not with your arms and legs.

Chapter 21

Open-Water Practice

Each summer, I divide my swimming between an outdoor 50-meter pool in New Paltz, and several lakes in the nearby Shawangunk Mountains. At the pool, I swim at slack times, with no lane lines so I sometimes have to weave through other bathers, providing "open-water practice" of a sort. I further simulate open-water in the pool by doing of the following:

Swimming "blind." Swimming 50-meters without lane lines tests how straight I swim when not following a line. As I take 30 to 40 strokes per length, I may swim 20-plus strokes with my eyes closed and see how far I've wandered from the line where I started. This will help me pick a frequency for sighting when I race.

Sighting. Once or twice each length, I can breathe and sight to the front, specifically practicing my ability to maintain balance and rhythm as I do. I can combine this with blind swimming — opening my eyes only when I lift my head — for an even more accurate simulation of the open water experience. (More guidance below.)

Drafting. I sometimes "draft" a few friends to swim with me and we practice close-order drafting, swimming in tight single file down the pool, with the leader dropping to the end at each wall. (More detail to follow.)

Porpoise. At the shallower end of the pool, I (or we) can begin the length with 3 or 4 porpoises before we begin stroking. We work on efficient, low-angle porpoising — channeling energy forward as we dive toward the bottom and back toward the surface, and on grabbing the bottom and pushing off quickly.

At one lake, I swim with a dozen or so triathletes (most wearing wetsuits), which offers the opportunity to rehearse situations I might encounter in a race. Each lake crossing is nearly 400 meters; we cross 6 to 8 times each session. I choose a specific focus for each crossing, which gives my lake practice far more value than if I just swam for time or distance. Here are the important ones:

Look This Way

Without a line to follow, any swimmer will eventually travel in a circle; the best swimmers in a 10-mile circle, others within the turning radius of a VW. In open water, you stay the course by occasionally sighting on landmarks, buoys, or swim caps. Practice can help you do that without losing your balance and flow. Here's what I practice:

Rock jetties and posts can make excellent landmarks.

Look less often. When your technique improves, you'll swim straighter. I often swim considerable distances without looking. It usually takes me about 320 strokes to cross the lake (yes, I count even there), so I'll often begin by taking 100 "blind" strokes (without checking my bearings) to see how straight I swim. If I've gone considerably off, I'll take fewer strokes before looking again. This gives me a sense of how often to sight in a race.

Sight smart. As we swim westward, our target is a dead tree angled into the water. Coming east, we swim toward a dock. Complicating the westward trip is sun glare that obscures the dead tree until we move into shadow, about 50 meters from the shore. How do I sight for the first 350 meters? On the bluff above the shore the treeline dips slightly just right of the spot we're aiming for. So I sight on the dip in the treeline until we reach the shadows. Heading east, the dock isn't clearly visible until the last 100 meters, so I use two buildings behind it, one a bit to its right and one to its left, to "triangulate." While warming up for a race, check for landmarks and other features that can help guide you when visibility is compromised.

Sight seamlessly. Sometimes the lake is almost as calm as pool water. When it is, I practice "surfing" my goggles barely over the surface, using my extending arm for support as I lift my head up and forward. Staying that low is far less tiring than holding my head aloft for several strokes in a row, but I may not get a completely clear picture. This sighting style is so easy to fit into my normal stroke rhythm that if I didn't get a complete picture, I assemble one by taking a series of "snapshots." And when windchop kicks up on the lake, I adjust by lifting just a bit higher or by taking more snapshots. These techniques help me maintain seamless balance and flow.

Stay low as you "surf" your goggles barely over the surface.

Breathe This Way

Breathing to both sides is a key skill for open water. Breathing to one side for 20 minutes or longer can leave neck and back muscles tense; breathing both ways keeps you looser. Second, you never know on which side your landmarks or buoys may be. And finally, waves, chop, or splashy swimmers on one side can be a problem unless you're comfortable breathing the other way. Fortunately, our TI Lessons should have helped you become comfortable with bilateral breathing. I do most of my swimming, in both pool and lake, breathing alternately. That could mean breathing every three strokes or every five if I'm going super slow (my effort level is low and so is my oxygen consumption). It could mean breathing on the right side while heading west and on the left going east. It could mean 10 breaths on my right, followed by 10 on my left. I practice all kinds of alternating patterns, so I can shift easily while racing.

In rougher water, lift the head a bit higher but keep one arm extended.

Lifting your head higher than necessary will lead to fatigue.

Practice Free Rides

Swimming just behind someone else can be worth as much as 10 percent in energy savings. Just as helpful, you can let your draftees do the work of navigation while you simply follow in their wake — but do check their bearings from time to time. I practice drafting in the pool, as I said, and at the lake, where I sometimes start at the back of the pack to practice drafting. I'll do my no-look strokes, and practice following other swimmers without actually looking for them. I try to sense their proximity by feeling the bubbles from their kick. You can also catch a ride by swimming alongside another swimmer (or between two swimmers) but close enough to stay within their bow wave, by keeping your goggles somewhere between their knees and feet. When drafting that way you can keep your "rabbit" in view with normal side-breathing.

After swimming "blind" for 40 or more strokes, I'll sneak a quick peak at my draftee's cap or for the center of the cluster of caps. Another way to use the pack to stay on course is by swimming to one side. If you know, for instance, that you typically wander to the left while swimming, position yourself to the right of most of the pack. Everyone else will help keep you in line.

*In this example, the swimmer on
the right is getting a more powerful drafting
advantage than the swimmer on the left.*

Swimming just behind someone can be
worth as much as 10% in energy savings.

Practice with Purpose

In addition to the gear-changing and timed pool sets outlined in Chapters 15 and 16, in the lake I test and develop my ability to stay smooth at racing speeds with a variety of pacing games. I will generally swim in a range of three "gears." **Silent** is virtually effortless. **Cruise** is a bit faster with some feeling of pace. **Brisk** represents the effort and pace I'd usually feel in the course of a mile race — but my race is complete after I swim so this pace may be a bit faster than most triathletes would want to swim. Here's a sample "lake workout" to show the range of creativity that is possible. Each "set" represents one "lake lap" — just under 400 meters.

Swim Super Slow and Silent. I try for the lowest possible stroke count and try to cross with fewer than four "looks."

Speedplay. Alternate rounds of 40 strokes Silent with 20 strokes Cruise. Try to be just as quiet and splash-free as you accelerate to "cruise pace."

SSP. Alternate thinking about hiding your head and timing your switches, with purposeful exaggeration. Count strokes.

Speedplay. Alternate 50 Silent strokes — 10 Cruise strokes, 40 Silent — 20 Cruise, 30 Silent — 30 Cruise, 20 Silent — 40 Cruise, 10 Silent — 50 Cruise. Be just as smooth for 50 strokes of Cruise as you are for 10.

*Let the lead swimmer(s) do the work of drafting
(and sighting) while you stay low and follow in their wake.*

Drafting practice. Start at the rear and practice "feeling wakes" and not looking very often. Also practice how to advance within the pack by leapfrogging from the "free ride" of one wake to the free ride of another wake further ahead in the pack, like a trout working upstream from rock to rock.

Speedplay. Alternate 20 strokes Silent — 20 strokes Cruise — 20 strokes Brisk. Try to stay just as smooth and fluent at Brisk as at Silent. You can also practice adjusting your tempo in the core, by keeping keep your arms connected to your faster-moving torso as you cycle through this repeatedly.

Pickups. Start at the rear of the pack, give the leaders a bit of a head start, then build your tempo and pace steadily across the lake, from Silent through Cruise, Brisk, and finally to full speed in the final 50 meters or so. This lap is a microcosm of a whole race, distilled to 400 meters.

Really Open Water

*Body surfing provides the perfect opportunity
for mastering sea skills while having fun.*

Ocean swimming is a whole different story. The best way to become comfortable and adept is to spend some time body surfing. It provides a perfect opportunity for mastering sea skills while having fun. Body surfing teaches you to be completely at ease in the ocean and particularly to understand waves. Swimming through breakers takes strength, wit, and timing. You can't just mash through them; they'll throw you back, gasping and muddled. Body surfing is ideal practice because after each ride in, you can't wait to catch another, so you learn to zip through the shore break quickly, with energy intact to grab your next ride.

Here's how to do it. Start in ankle-deep water and high-step through the shallows, leaping over low rollers. Ocean bottom is notoriously unpredictable (a hole here, a sand bar there), so watch your step. But you probably won't run far anyway, unless the tide is way out; it's easier to porpoise once the water covers your knees. Dive forward, grab the sand, and pull your feet under you. Plant your feet, then dive up and over to arc back toward the bottom again. Each time you pop up, immediately look for the next wave. When depth makes this awkward or laborious, start swimming. But you have to check the wave line every two or three strokes.

High-step over low rollers

Dive through the base of the wave just before it breaks

*As these three swimmers practice ins and outs, they
demonstrate three stages of getting into the water:*

If you see a shoulder forming that looks as if it could break, you're probably over a sand bar. Try to get your feet down and prepare to dive under the wave. The ideal time, if you're fortunate enough, is to dive through the base of the wave just before it breaks. That will actually shoot you out the back with added momentum. If you can't manage that, just duck under before it reaches you.

Or, you may be facing 30 yards or more of rollers that broke farther out and are coming at you in lines, usually in water too deep to porpoise. Sometimes you may be able to take only a few strokes before another wave is on top of you, forcing you to dive again. Leave one arm in front as you breathe, swing the other arm over, and drive it in strongly as you pike under. Breaststroke once quickly and resurface, looking immediately for the next wave. Get in as many strokes as you can to power through the white water behind them, ready to dive under again. It can be difficult to get a rhythm going; you really need to be comfortable with being buffeted and thrown off your stride every few strokes, then resuming your rhythm quickly. As I said, there is absolutely no substitute for practicing this a lot.

Once you're past the breaker line, you'll be swimming in chop or swells of some height. Practice comes in handy here, too, because it helps you learn to sense when you're riding up on a crest or sinking in a trough. There's no point in sighting while in a trough. With experience, you learn to time your looks for when you feel yourself rising on a swell. In July of 2000, I swam a mile race in storm surf where the swells ranged upward of five feet, which limited the size of the field and scattered it considerably. Most of the time I swam blindly in what I hoped was the right direction, pausing frequently to take two to four breast strokes, hoping to catch a glimpse of another swim cap. When I saw one, I'd swim that way, anxious for company out in the wet-and-wildness. In any sort of chop, which is common in the ocean, it helps enormously to have had considerable experience getting your bearings. You need to learn to time the waves, and to perhaps delay a breath (or breathe to the other side) because you can sense a wave about to slap you in the face. Another option worth practicing is to take a deep breath to your side, then look up and spot without swallowing water as a wave splashes over you.

I know it can sound scary but, in time, you essentially learn to roll with the punches, to trust your swimming ability and the safety measures of the race organizers and to relax and find a rhythm in harmony with the swells around you. Three adjustments can be particularly helpful in a choppy sea. First, swing your arms a bit higher on recovery. Second, roll farther to breathe — just as far as you need to find air. Finally, be intently focused on *piercing* the waves, rather than bullying your way through them.

In choppy seas swing your arms a bit higher on recovery.

Stay low but roll farther to breathe.

At some point, you'll need to return to shore. If there's a shore break of any size, it will definitely occur to you that you might get *crushed* by a wave sneaking up from behind. A swimmer who knows how to ride waves and how to "read" the ebb and flow of a breaker line can get to shore much faster and more smoothly. Once you've cleared the final buoy and are headed toward shore, don't worry too much about finishing your swim right in front of the finish line. Instead of angling toward the finish line while swimming, swim straight in and then run along the shore to the swim finish. You'll get there much faster by running than by swimming diagonally *and* you'll handle the shore break much better going straight in.

Once you are in the *breaker zone* again, you'll feel this: A swell will catch up with you and you'll feel your body accelerating. *Swim faster*, using the boost for as long as you can. Once the wave passes you, you'll feel yourself being pulled back in the ebb. *Work hard enough to counter this*, then resume your normal rhythm again. Finally, you'll be close enough to shore that you can sense waves beginning to break. Now is a good time to turn on your back for a few strokes to see if there's one you can catch. When you feel yourself being sucked into a breaking wave, rotate to face down and swim three to four strokes at top speed, then put one or both arms forward, put your head down, and lean on your chest as you keep kicking.

Keep kicking and leaning on your leading arm for as long as you feel yourself in the wave. When it passes, if you can feel the bottom as you stroke, start porpoising. If the tide is out and there's a long shallow zone between the break and the beach, throw yourself ahead of following waves as they catch up to you. It's easier to catch a mini ride than to run and leap through knee-deep shore break.

How to practice this? Simple and fun. More body surfing. Most of the time you won't be at the shoreline at the end of your ride, so you can practice porpoising, mini rides, and high-stepping out of the water. Another good form of practice at the beach is to set up a mini-course, repeatedly swimming out 50 yards or so and then returning, always starting and finishing on shore.

*If you can feel the bottom
as you stroke, start porpoising.*

In the 1970s, I worked as a lifeguard at Jones Beach State Park on Long Island. At Field Six, where I was stationed, we would set up a mini course by anchoring a milk or bleach jug about 75 yards from the main stand. On down time, we would often practice several dashes into the surf, stroking out to the buoy and then back to shore, finishing each by running to the stand. Whenever the surf was up, we'd spend hours body surfing. It was exhilarating fun — as well as invaluable practice of our rescue skills. I've loved racing in the ocean ever since.

Start to run in ankle-deep water.

Swim Safely

If you're not fortunate, as I am, to have a group to practice with, don't swim unprotected. Ask someone to swim with you or to paddle or row along. If your swimming partner is less experienced, keep an eye on him or her while you swim. If you swim where there's motorboat or jet-ski traffic, you *must* have an escort boat, and you should always swim with a bright-colored cap. Otherwise, swim on a guarded beach. One of my practice sites, Lake Awosting, offers an enclosed-and-guarded area about 50 meters wide. I practice all of the same skills mentioned above, while crossing back and forth for 40 minutes or more. If you swim in an unfamiliar spot, learn all you can about conditions: currents and riptides, submerged rocks or pilings.

Chapter 22

Putting It All Together on Race Day

You drive into the parking area. It's not even 6:30, and the morning chill won't dissipate for another hour or two. You shrink from the thought of leaving the warmth of your car for water that will feel even colder. You also recall your last race, when you stepped in a hole on the start and fell on your face while everyone splashed past. Still you got up immediately and plunged into a churn of arms, legs, and bodies all the way to the first buoy, where somehow the crowd thickened as five other swimmers tried to squeeze into space for one and your goggles came askew. Finally, you got on course...sort of...because you couldn't see the buoys and feared you were wandering blindly with few clues as to how far you had swum or how much of this unpleasant ordeal remained. After what seemed like forever — and with an extra quart or two of swallowed water — you stumbled on shore (tripping once more) and dragged yourself to the transition area. You have no trouble finding your bike; most of the field was long gone. You stare out the windshield and the thought crosses your mind: "Maybe I should just stick with duathlons."

I expect quite a few of you will shake your head in rueful recognition at this slightly exaggerated account. I've been racing in open water for nearly 30 years and all of this has happened to me, at one time or another. I admit to cringing momentarily at leaving my car to plunge into cold water first thing in the morning. But, mixed with that unease is the anticipation any runner feels upon arriving at a road race and seeing all the other runners preparing. Without exception, every race I've done has left me euphoric — about overcoming reluctance, the elements, and the unique challenges of open water. Even as I sit at my desk writing about it, I can feel anticipation and excitement rising for the fun I expect to have racing again. So, here's some advice on how to cut the challenges down to size and allow your strengths to come to the fore.

Pre-Race Reconnaissance

Pack extra goggles so a broken strap won't throw you. I use Seal goggles (see Resources for info) because of their extraordinary visibility, and bring one pair each of mirrored and clear. I'll use the mirrored if sun glare appears to be a factor; otherwise, it's the clear. I also pack a small tube of toothpaste or bottle of baby shampoo. I smear a small amount inside my goggles then wash and wipe it off when I first enter the water. Both are effective anti-fog agents. I also pack Vaseline or Body Glide. I get underarm chafing in open water — especially in salt water — if I don't lubricate first. Finally, I drink-and-drive...water or dilute Gatorade, that is. Because there won't be any water stops during the race, I hydrate steadily on my way to the race and up until the start.

Arrive early, allowing ample time to check in and set up your transitions. After setting up your bike, ask the lifeguards about wave height, currents, or sweep if you are swimming in the ocean. Unless it's a short course (600 meters or less), you probably won't swim the entire course during warmup. But you can rehearse it creatively. Read the course map and study the course from shore. What shape is it? How many buoys mark it? Are turn buoys a different size or color than those between turns? On which side of the buoys do you need to swim?

If you have the inclination for a pre-race dip, wade out and examine the swim finish from the water. Take a mental snapshot of how the finish area and path to transition will look — *through your goggles*. Then jog easily from shore toward knee-depth water and back several times to learn bottom conditions — sand, rocks, weeds, mud or muck — and decide where you'll stop running and begin to porpoise, on the way out and on the way in. Next, practice a few ins and outs. Starting from ankle-deep water, rehearse the sequence of run-porpoise-swim. After 10 strokes, turn around and do it in reverse. Swim in until your hands scrape the bottom, then switch to porpoise, and finally jog to shore. Two or three of these will provide priceless intelligence.

Warmup

I like to do a fair bit of swimming before I race, so after a few ins and outs, I swim easily to the first buoy to see how the course will look once I round it and whether there are landmarks on the horizon. I also note the position of the sun and whether it will help or hinder visibility. If the final buoy is nearby, I'll swim over to it and see how the finish line will look as I head for home. Remember that the position of the sun will be different by the time you finish.

Another important part of my preparation is to do roughly 200 meters of SSPs, to choose focal points for the race. This prepares me physically by tuning up my muscles and nervous system and helps customize my preparation to race conditions. If the water is flat, I might focus on hiding my head and swimming taller. If there's windchop, I might focus on rotation and *piercing* the water. Rehearsing SSPs can also be an effective way to block out pre-race anxiety. Jitters arise from dwelling on things we can't control. By practicing SSPs in warmup, you shift your focus to narrow technical points that you *can* control, blocking out distractions.

The final part of my warmup will be 200 meters or so of speedplay like those I practiced in Williams Lake (and similar to the pickups runners do in warmup): 20 strokes Silent, 20 Cruise, 20 Silent, 20 Brisk — perhaps two rounds. I try to do just enough to "cue" my nervous system for the task ahead, but not so many that I feel fatigue. This is another narrowly focused activity that will keep nerves at bay and help you dial in the race flow you'd like when the starting horn sounds.

Race starts are often in waves and, at my age, I'm usually in the third or fourth. After the wave ahead of mine starts, if I have five minutes and the starter permits, I'll keep swimming easily near the starting line, checking my watch every 30 to 40 strokes until about a minute remains, then move into position for the start. The continued swimming helps keep fresh how I want my stroke to feel in the race. It also keeps me focused and calm and warmer than if I stood and shivered with the other swimmers.

The Start

If you have limited open-water racing experience or feel even moderate anxiety about it, you'll be far more comfortable starting off to one side. As much open-water experience as I have, if the start is crowded, I look for open space. If there's a sweep or current, I start upsweep of the pack. On Long Island, the ocean sweep runs east to west, so I start toward the eastern edge of the group. The sweep will carry me toward the first buoy while I swim out fairly straight.

Still feeling jittery and unsure as you stand there? Nervous excitement is only natural, but just take a good look around. Note the lifeguards clustered offshore waiting for you. They'll take good care of you, help keep you on course, and be at your side quickly if you need them. Then survey your fellow athletes; they'll be out there all around you, and the ones you're most likely to be swimming with probably match up with you pretty well. And they're all feeling the same jitters. Besides, after following the program in this book, you're better prepared than most. Finally, look inward: YOU'RE Fishlike; you've prepared thoroughly and all you need do now is swim as you've practiced.

Unless the course is 400 meters or less, the race won't be decided in the first 100 meters. If it's at least one kilometer, you can take your time finding a comfortable pace. How comfortably you swim will hugely influence how you feel on the bike and run, and the first 100 to 200 meters will largely determine your comfort in the swim. If you have more racing experience and a fairly developed stroke, you can start with 40 to 80 fairly brisk strokes. Don't sight or look. Just follow all those bodies ahead of you.

In the first 200 meters, let yourself be carried by the energy of the pack; use your arms to carve out a space amongst the thrashing arms and legs. The tightest swarm of bodies is the knot trying to round the first buoy. Swim about five yards outside to avoid them, take a good look at where everyone is heading, and then fall in behind them at the pace and rhythm you'll maintain most of the race. If somehow your goggles get kicked off, roll to your back and kick easily while adjusting them.

One more thing about starts: In water temperatures in the 60s or lower, it's common to experience a gasp reflex during the first few strokes. The water literally takes your breath away. Even top athletes aren't immune. If you feel yourself gasping, just slow down. Do a few strokes of breaststroke or turn onto your back. But don't stop entirely. Movement helps; just take slower strokes until you feel normal breathing return.

Navigating and Drafting

During the first quarter of the race you'll probably see quite a few caps ahead of you. No worries; that just gives you more of a guide for navigating. Aim for the middle of the cluster. And each time you look up, don't be surprised if there are fewer caps out there. This usually happens without your having to pursue them. Just keep moving steadily and people will come back to you as they fatigue.

You'll find it far easier to maintain balance and flow if you try to swim 25 yards (20 strokes) without looking up. As your confidence and form improve, you can extend this to 50 or more strokes. When you do look, keep your weight shifted forward to minimize drag and maintain balance. Your wetsuit helps too. Before looking, try to picture what you should see when you look, and this doesn't mean just buoys or caps. Use the angle of the sun, piers, buildings or trees on shore, lifeguards on their rescue boards, boats at anchor.

You can draft by swimming alongside someone's knees.

To save even more energy, follow others closely and let *them* sight for you. If there is an occasion to draft, take it, either feeling for the bubbles from someone's kick or looking at their legs alongside as you breathe. If you're comfortable and not feeling *way* too slow, just stay there so long as the occasion remains, contemplating happily how the folks in front are reducing drag and saving you energy. Move cunningly from one drafting opportunity to another, like a trout heading upstream, resting for a bit behind one rock before swimming to the next rock. Between drafting opportunities, focus on minimizing drag by slipping through the smallest space in the water, and on keeping a steady core rhythm, your arms connected to your core.

Regroup in Sweet Spot when you need a rest.

If, for some reason, you feel any discomfort out there, mental or physical, or feel your heart rate rising, try any of the following: Begin counting strokes to occupy your mind. Focus on an SSP to put flow in your stroke. Roll to your Sweet Spot, kicking easily for a bit, and regroup. Being in Sweet Spot, particularly with a wetsuit, should be very relaxing. Remember, Sweet Spot is your "wall" any time you need one, in open water.

Finishing

Unless there's a clear turnaround that tells you the race is half over, you'll usually have only a vague idea how much of the race is complete. Unlike in a pool race in which the lap counter constantly alerts you how far you've gone and how much remains, in open water you can lose your sense of time and distance. You'll need to be more cautious in your pacing than you would be with distance markers. Try to increase your pace by tiny amounts as the race goes along (regular Speedplay practice will give you an internal "speedometer"), but never increase your pace or intensity unless you're certain you can sustain it and build on it through the end of the race. And *don't give a thought* to picking up the pace if you are in a triathlon and must bike and run after you reach shore. Just stay smooth and happily reflect on how fresh you'll feel when you mount your bicycle.

Jog or walk calmly to the transition area,
unzipping your wetsuit as you go.

When you finish the swim, don't rush to the transition area. I watched Mark Allen walk up the ramp at the swim finish of the Hawaiian Ironman in almost a leisurely fashion — thinking, no doubt, that another 7 hours of hard racing remained — as others around him scrambled hurriedly out of the water. He went on to win easily. So, at best, *jog* calmly from the beach to the transition area, unzipping and peeling your wet-suit to the waist as you go. Since I've worn a wetsuit only once — and removed it laboriously — my best advice is to practice taking yours off to work out the easiest way to shed your neoprene skin. Once you reach your bike, start re-hydrating immediately, since you've not been able to drink while swimming.

At this point, my work is done, but yours is just beginning. Now the real race starts. Enjoy it; you should have all the energy you need to give it your best.

Afterword

Now Take Your Swimming to Unexpected Places

My daughter Cari plays Ultimate Frisbee at Wesleyan University. I went last weekend to watch her play in a tournament. It looked like exhilarating fun, but later she mentioned that she'd never touched the disk during the game. Because, like me, she's not a born athlete, and frisbee is often a coed game, most of the other players were faster, stronger or able to jump higher. Cari wistfully related the thrill of watching a player from another school race from one side of the end zone to the other, dive headlong, somersault and *then* snatch the disk inches from the turf for a one-of-a-kind, acrobatic score. "I know I'll never be a human highlight film," she said "but I still think I can become a good player and I think the way to do that is to work on my throwing."

Smart thinking. She'd pinpointed a key part of the game that doesn't require special physical talents, but will accede to patient, diligent practice. If she is simply willing to spend hours mastering the countless ways one can artfully snap one's wrist to deliver a disk to the precise spot a streaking teammate will be at a particular moment in time — while also learning to *read* an unfolding play to anticipate opportunities — she could become a masterful playmaker. And as she does, she may experience exquisite satisfaction — not just because frisbee-tossing is fun, but from the satisfaction of seeing her ability to make the disk do what she wishes steadily increase. But most of all, she has a good chance to achieve the blissful state created by having mind and body fully engaged in mastering a challenging skill.

Having completed the basic aim of this book: to provide practical tools to help you swim better in a triathlon or open-water — I now invite you to go one step further and experience what has been the most satisfying and instructive aspect of swimming for me — that it is almost ideally suited to revealing the pleasures of the pursuit of Mastery.

What is Mastery?

Mastery is the intriguing process during which what was once difficult becomes progressively easier and more pleasurable through practice. Whenever we witness some form of memorably high-level performance–whether it's Isaac Stern on the violin, an acrobatic frisbee player, or Ian Thorpe in the pool — we instinctively assume that mastery requires some sort of inborn genius. But mastery is not just for the fortunate few; *anyone* who pursues a personally-challenging goal — no matter how modest their starting point — can experience its rewards

Swimming is a uniquely fitting medium for cultivating the habits of mastery because it is the antithesis of a genetically programmed activity. When we do it instinctively, by and large, we do it very poorly. Yet, while human DNA may not be ideal for swimming, it *is* encoded to learn prodigiously from birth to death. And it is the mastery of skills for which we are not genetically programmed that differentiate us from all other creatures.

Swimming mastery is not about swimming 100 meters under a minute or a 2.4-mile Ironman swim leg under an hour; it's not even really about achieving some level of stroke efficiency. It's about uniting mind and body, without distraction and boredom, in patient, focused, almost loving, practice. Practice of this sort can teach you how to learn and perform in almost anything.

The first of these lessons is the value of long-term dedication to the journey itself. If there is any sure route to personal fulfillment, it is in valuing the patient journey toward mastery over the desire for quick and easy results. Cultivate modest expectations along the way and every time you reach a benchmark or breakthrough, enjoy it, then keep practicing, hoping you will always have some further plateau to aim for.

Learning to love routine

An essential insight for achieving mastery is that learning any challenging skill involves brief spurts forward, followed by a much longer plateau slightly higher than the previous one. To pursue Mastery, you must embrace the idea of spending most of your time on a plateau, continuing to practice enthusiastically even when you seem to be stagnating. Those occasional upward surges are not the only time progress is occurring. On an invisible, cellular level, learning and adaptation are constant, so long as you are giving your body tasks that require deep concentration to complete.

And you keep yourself on the path toward mastery by practicing primarily *for the sake of practice itself.* Rather than becoming frustrated by your seeming lack of progress, learn to appreciate your daily practice routine, just as much as you are thrilled by the periodic breakthrough. Just as Zen practice does, your swimming practice can bring peace and serenity by filling the space usually occupied by the problems and distractions of your external life.

Every time I enter a pool, I immediately enter a blissful sense of well-being, because it's proven to be one of the few areas of life in which I can consistently do just what I want. That sense of peace allows me to luxuriate in incremental progress. At the end of every year I know I'm swimming better than the year before, stroke counts slightly lower, fluency slightly greater. And perhaps once a year I get an electrifying moment of clarity or insight. But the routine between those moments is never boring because I feel I am never more fully myself than when working on mastery. The pleasure I have gained from swimming this way has led me to other activities — rowing, yoga, cross-country skiing — that offer similar opportunities for incremental improvement through mindful practice. Together they provide an encouraging sense that, even at age 50, I'm getting steadily better as an athlete.

The *Tao* of Practice

Just before the 2000 Olympics, I read an illuminating profile of Marion Jones, who was on her way to gold medals in sprints and hurdles. I can't recall the writer's name, but I took these notes: "She was endowed with the neurological on-off switches to take 47 steps in less than 11 seconds with no loss of power (the average person can take about 35)...Grueling conditioning helps. So does obsessive attention to the smallest details. Running 100 meters is a violent act, beginning with a gunshot. At the same time, the training involved is analogous to a concert pianist's mastering Chopin; both are performances that require ferocious concentration and a fanatical regimen that reduces learned muscular actions to nearly automatic responses.... She trains with punctilious precision, systematically solving tiny biomechanical problems that keep her from running fractionally faster than anyone else." The writer describes a training session: "I mostly see her stepping over 10 hurdles set three feet apart...and that's about all she is doing for the better part of three hours...drilling it into both mind and body...to maintain perfect posture, which helps to keep her feet below the center of mass, which helps her explode through the hips."

Marion Jones's practice sounds very much like the *learning* and *practice* forms I suggested in Chapters 12 and 13, but radically different from conventional grind-it-out swim training. This is what differentiates *practice* from a *workout*. For anyone on the master's journey, the word practice is not just something you *do*, but is akin to the Chinese word *tao*, which means path. A practice is anything you immerse yourself in as an integral part of your life. You practice skilled swimming, not just to swim faster, but for the inherent pleasure it brings.

Sports psychologist Dr. Bob Rotella observed that the best golfers on the PGA Tour, spend more time on the practice tee than less successful players. Are they best because they practice so much or do they practice so much because of the pressure or responsibility of being the best? Rotella learned, after interviewing them, that their primary motivation for practice was the sheer pleasure of performing at the peak of their abilities. Because they swing a golf club with such exquisite control, they are happy to spend hour upon hour doing it. And the volume and complete engagement of their practice reinforces their skills and dominance. Finally, the more their skills increase, the more they enjoy practice; the essence of a positive addiction.

A few of our students have shown an impatience to move from simple drills to advanced drills to swimming to swimming *fast*. In contrast, the most advanced TI practitioners, like Don Walsh, the TI Master Teacher and champion marathon swimmer I mentioned in Chapter 7, who have been practicing the drills for years, have learned to appreciate the subtleties and endless possibilities contained within even the most rudimentary techniques.

On occasion, Don may repeat a single drill for 30 minutes or more. The uninterrupted, meditative repetition expands his awareness significantly. What start out as barely noticeable variations in execution become significant and revealing and can be tweaked with much more subtlety. This is why Tiger Woods can swing a golf club for six or eight hours a day without a moment of boredom. He experiences and examines so much more in every swing than does the ordinary golfer that it offers an incredible richness of experience. This newness — new insights, new awareness in "old" skills and movements — banishes boredom and impatience forever.

Becoming a Master

As I said earlier, the rewards of mastery are not reserved only for those gifted with special talents. The process of practicing like a Master will enable you to achieve a higher level of excellence and a deeper sense of satisfaction. Here are several tools to help you start your journey:

Knowledge is Power

When spending your precious time at practice — and to commit yourself without reservation — it's essential that you be confident you're on the right path. If I have done my job well, this book — confirmed by your body's feedback — can be your source of that certainty. I expect that most of those who read this book will be self-coached, but a devoted student armed with knowledge, is better off than a student with a poor teacher. And even if you have a coach, the ultimate responsibility for progress toward Mastery lies not with your teacher but with you.

Videotapes can be a source of guidance and information. If a picture is worth 1000 words, then a moving picture is probably worth 10,000 words. But learning is immeasurably aided by feedback. And you can create feedback for yourself when a teacher isn't available by finding a practice partner.

Build a support system

You can work toward mastery on your own, but it helps to share the journey with others: People who have gone through the same process and can share their wisdom and insight. People who are on the path at the same time as you, so you can compare notes. People who are simply interested in your well-being and growth and will offer encouragement. Finally, you can recruit a practice partner. Share your knowledge and goals with them and invite them to join you on the path to mastery. You'll gain a better understanding of what you have been working on learning if you teach some part of it to a partner...and they will then be better equipped to help you right back.

Emotional equilibrium

Eugen Herrigel, in his book *Zen in the Art of Archery*, wrote that zen archers do not train primarily to shoot bullseyes, but to increase their self-understanding. Similarly, mastery is not a pursuit of perfection, but of self-knowledge — including your flaws and limitations. You'll never reach perfection anyway, and that's fortunate, because, you'll always have some higher goal inspiring you. And particularly in swimming, so long as you have Human DNA, you will never exhaust your opportunities for learning or improvement. Further, it's *essential* to feel clumsy or incompetent at times — and to smile at yourself when you do. The understanding of a master learner is measured by their willingness to surrender what they "know" in order to learn something new. When teaching a four-stroke camp, we observed that experienced backstrokers struggled far more with a new backstroke drill than those who were inexperienced in backstroke. Because they "knew" how backstroke should feel, they insisted on fitting this drill into that experience. The novices achieved fluency in the drill quickly. The experienced ones began to approach the same fluency only when they allowed themselves to "forget" what they knew about backstroke. And they were soon swimming backstroke better than ever.

Use *all your potentiality*

In his influential book, *Tao of Jeet Kune Do*, Bruce Lee wrote that 10 minutes of practice with mind and body fully integrated is worth more than 10 hours of going through the motions. It's well known that most humans operate at only a tiny fraction of their true potential and that the key to realizing more of that potential is mental, not physical. When Jack Nicklaus was the world's dominant golfer, he revealed that he never hit a shot without first visualizing the ball's perfect flight and successful conclusion "sitting up there high and white and pretty on the green." Mindful practice in swimming will soon give you an archive of "mental movies," as captivating as Nicklaus's. Driving home from practice, you may find yourself reliving the pleasure of a rhythmic, fluid stroke. Impressions like these provide the basis for detailed recall and rehearsal of the way "great" swimming feels — or of the way it looks, after watching some masterful swimmer. As you become more Fishlike, practices and races can become so enjoyable that you'll find yourself replaying them, recalling the pleasures of fluid movement hours later, just as you relive other pleasant memories. These will give you a powerful tool for reinforcing the physical part of learning. Soon, your "warmup" (both for practice and races) will become as much mental as physical. Your imagery will begin to prime your nervous system as you "swim on your way to the pool."

Making the path to mastery a powerful habit will enrich the totality of your life experience. Though you began with the limited goal of swimming better in a triathlon, you can go well beyond that to making swimming a deeply satisfying experience to learning life lessons that can enrich nearly any valued undertaking.

Happy laps,
Terry Laughlin
New Paltz NY
October, 2001

Resources

www.totalimmersion.net

The TI website will be your most valuable source of support and information. Important features include:

- A free newsletter featuring new highly-focused, immediately useful articles each week. A key ingredient of this newsletter will be articles contributed by TI learners like you, sharing the insights that have helped them reach their goals. Please consider becoming a contributor.

- An ongoing discussion forum for triathletes who are using this book and TI methods to improve their swimming. Use this forum to share your insights, discoveries and successes, to ask questions and to tap the experience of others who are on the same mastery path as you. This forum will be a Learning Community for smart triathlon swimming.

- Samples of TI-specific practices for both technique improvement and effective training

- A steadily-growing directory of trained and certified TI Coaches available to work with you toward achievement of your goals and complete swimming fulfillment.

- Information on how YOU can become a certified TI teacher-coach. You may have realized how difficult it can be to find a coach who can help you with TI practice. You can be part of the solution. Most of our certified teachers started like you, by learning TI, realizing how simple and effective it was, and wanting to share their discovery with others. Most had never before thought of teaching swimming.

Fishlike Freestyle the Total Immersion Way

This video was designed specifically as a companion to this book. Visual reinforcement is priceless in learning physical skills. Organized into the same six lessons you'll find in Chapter 10. Order at www.totalimmersion.net, or by calling 800-609-7946, or use the order form included in this book.

From my bookshelf

Six well-thumbed titles from my bookshelf have been a priceless source of guidance to me on staying strong and supple at age 50 (or any other age.)

Staying Supple by John Jerome, Breakaway Books

The Supple Body by Sara Black, Macmillan Books

Stretching by Bob Anderson, Shelter Publications

Yoga Mind and Body, DK Publishing, Inc.

The Pilates Body by Brooke Siler, Broadway Books

Body Control, The Pilates Way by Lynne Robinson and Gordon Thompson, Pan Macmillan Books UK

Total Immersion Products

Total Immersion offers weekend workshops year round and nationwide, as well as videos, books, website, and more than a dozen carefully chosen products that we believe will truly improve your swimming. To order any of our products or to enroll in a Total Immersion weekend workshop, call **800-609-7946** (845-256-9770 from outside the USA) or visit us online at **www.totalimmersion.net**.

Video: Fishlike Freestyle the Total Immersion Way
You don't have the companion video yet? What are you waiting for? As I said, you'll learn faster and easier with video to guide you. Not convinced yet? Try it for a month, on us. If it's not the most effective swim-instruction video ever, send it back for an unconditional full refund.

Swimming Made Easy
If you've been encouraged with your success at learning freestyle, learn all the strokes the TI way with SME. Swimming different strokes is the swimming equivalent of cross-training. New skills = better freestyle = more enjoyment and longevity. *Get 40% off the cover price when you order with one or more of our videos.*

Video: Freestyle and Backstroke the Total Immersion Way
Video: Butterfly and Breaststroke the Total Immersion Way
See above. You'll learn faster and easier with video guides.

Laminated Drill Guides
The two "different strokes" videos just above are ideal for providing a dynamic sense of how TI drills should be performed. For each, we also offer waterproof POOL PRIMERS to take to the pool for more precise practice. Illustrated by surface and underwater pics on laminated pages, spiral bound for ease of use. Convenient 8" x 5" format. Unconditionally guaranteed, like everything we produce.

More tools for smart triathlon-swimmers.
See **http://www.totalimmersion.net/tsme.html** for Seal goggles, Fistgloves, Ironman wetsuits, fins and swimwear.

Notes

Notes

Notes

Notes

Notes

™

Notes